THE MAN IN THE MIRROR

CHRISTIAN FAITH SERIES
Reinhold Niebuhr, Consulting Editor

THE MAN
IN THE MIRROR

Studies in the Christian

Understanding of Selfhood

> Where I belong, and what I
> am living for, I first learned
> in the mirror of history.
> **KARL JASPERS**
>
> Man is the creature made vis-
> ible in the mirror of Jesus
> Christ.
> **KARL BARTH**

The William Belden Noble

Lectures for 1957 by

ALEXANDER MILLER

DOUBLEDAY & COMPANY, INC., GARDEN CITY, NEW YORK, 1958

The quotations on the title page are taken from Karl
Jaspers *The Origin and Goal of History*. New Haven.
Yale University Press. 1953. p. 271, and Karl Barth
Against The Stream. London. SCM Press. 1954. p.
185.

Library of Congress Catalog Card Number 58–10031

To Jean

PREFACE

The substance of these studies was delivered at Harvard University under the William Belden Noble Lectureship in December 1957. In establishing the Lectureship in 1906, the Founder declared her intention "to continue the mission of her husband, whose supreme desire was to extend the influence of Jesus as 'the Way, the Truth and the Life,' and to illustrate and enforce the words of Jesus—'I am come that they might have life and that they might have it more abundantly.' "

The lectures were directed to undergraduates, but the undergraduate is first of all, and in spite of occasional appearance, a human being; and it is hoped, therefore, that as now published they may speak to the human condition both within and beyond the university. The material is in some sense a development of the writer's *The Renewal of Man*, which was published under the same imprint in 1955.

I was greatly honored to undertake the Lectureship. Harvard is not only a historic center of liberal learning, but the center also of notable contemporary developments in the relation of Christian faith to liberal learning. I am personally indebted to the President of the University, to the chairman of the Board of Preachers, and to members of the faculty and student body for the warmth of their hospitality and the stimulus of their conversation.

9

We are about to see great days in the age-long relation of
the Church of Christ to the scholarly community, and in the
renewed integrity and vitality of the Community of Faith
both in this land and beyond it.

My prayer is that these studies may be of some Christian
use in this good cause.

ALEXANDER MILLER

Stanford University
Stanford, California

CONTENTS

THE MAN IN THE MIRROR

CHAPTER I

The Self's Knowledge of Itself

> Every man has forgotten who he is. One may
> understand the cosmos but never the ego;
> the ego is more distant than any star. Thou
> shalt love the Lord thy God, but thou shalt
> not know thyself. We are all under the same
> mental calamity; we have all forgotten our
> names. We have all forgotten who we really
> are. All that we call common sense and
> rationality and practicality and positivism
> only means that for certain dead levels of
> life we forget that we have forgotten. All that
> we call spirit and art and ecstasy only means
> that for one awful instant we remember that
> we forget.
>
> G. K. CHESTERTON[1]

The eminent Paul Tillich once convulsed a class at Union
Seminary by inquiring rhetorically: "What child has not
asked: why am I part of the totality of Being?" For Tillich
the ontological question is inevitable, and he himself has
been engaged with it, as he mildly explained, since the age
of six. I'm not sure how characteristic this is of children; but

there is some sign that it is pretty general among undergraduates. An actual undergraduate essay begins:

In the timelessness of the history of all men's lives, a great agonizing cry arises: "Who am I?"

For myself I'd be inclined to put this in *The New Yorker* category of "Cries That We Doubt Ever Got Cried." Most people are too absorbed in earning a living or gathering rosebuds to spare breath for what Karl Barth calls "existential screaming," though there are ample signs of hidden strain. But the more normal effect of the inturning of the present generation upon itself and the self's concerns is a brooding silence rather than an agonizing cry, and for this reason we have learned to speak of the present student generation, at any rate, as "the silent generation".

THE PRESENT PREOCCUPATION

Certainly on a superficial description there has been a shift from social and political activity to a concern with the self and its problems. Time was, it is said, when the undergraduate cut classes to cut capers on the soapbox and the picket line: now he either stays with his classwork for the professional percentage that's in it, or because he knows nothing important enough to pull him away. And outside of class he is more likely to be found in the intimate bull session than in the public and political demonstration.

Whatever substance there may be in this general account, I know that I myself precisely a generation ago spent hours that must have added up to months on soapboxes, contending for everything from pacifism to Prohibition. I still shun delights and live laborious days in an attempt to catch up on the scholarly and professional equipment I could have been accumulating during those days, had I not been parading with the unemployed and shouting for elemental justice on the street corners of New Zealand cities. I now happen to believe that some of the causes for which I then contended were false causes, and the arguments I used for them can still, in the recollection, bring a blush to these aging cheeks. But I learned a lot in contending for them, and after all if I had *not* contended for them I might still believe them, instead of moving on to that matured and seasoned wisdom of which you are now to have the benefit: if what I take for wisdom is not, as it well may be, simply the hardening of the spiritual arteries.

If it be true, even approximately, that that generation was passionate and this phlegmatic, that one vociferous and this one silent, the reasons are easy enough to come by. There is actually a good deal less human and social distress now than there was then, at least locally. Certain of the older problems seem to have found at least provisional solution, while those that remain (we talk of them in Chapter V) seem remote, complex, and unmanageable—hidden in the mysterious East and the impossible tangle of the Middle East. Then again, so many of the gods of that generation are now publicly labeled "Gods that Failed" that the credentials of all pretended gods are scrutinized a bit more cynically than was our habit. And the contemporary perception that "Hell is paved with good revolutions" has the effect of damping down insurrectionary ardor. The old, simple, heart-warming slogans seem no longer simple but rather simple-minded. Whatever the complex of causes, the effect in any event is silence, a silence which is at once the sign and the occasion of a brooding preoccupation with the problems of the interior life.

In *The Christian Century*[2] Charles Morris, talking about "Varieties of Human Value," says that undergraduates are at "the least religious period of life," a period in which, he seems to mean, the outgoing of religious devotion like the outgoing of political activity is contracted to a preoccupation with "finding and developing ourselves." Now this is odd: for not only have students from Paris 1200 to Budapest 1956 made a habit of breaking out of the circle of self-concern into all kinds of exhilarating activity, but in our own day the phrase "the least religious period" clashes with the accepted notion that students in general are in the process of having profound second thoughts about religion. The phrase "the religious revival in the colleges" has at least as much currency as "the silent generation."

The man has a point, but I should put it somewhat differently. The fact is that the resurgence of interest in religion and the concern about "finding and developing the self" tend to run together, so that "religion" becomes an instrument for self-understanding and self-mastery. The word of the ancient oracle: "Know thyself" takes on the force of a pious injunction. Self-knowledge for the sake of self-fulfillment is taken to be a religious objective:

> Resolve to be thyself, and know
> That he who finds himself loses his misery

as Matthew Arnold put it more succinctly.

There is enough truth here to make the thing seductive, but there is a snag to it. I have a continuing and somewhat critical connection with one of the large undergraduate religious conferences, which meets every year. The older leadership, which was trained most of a generation ago, injects a continuing concern about social questions; but the students who shape up the annual conference build their propaganda appeal on this preoccupation with the self, so that the over-all title of the conference is couched generally in some such form as *Who Am I? What Am I? I and My World* and, inevitably, *The World and I* (or is it *Me?*). The presumption is that the prerequisite of all knowledge and of all fruitful action is self-knowledge, and this sounds plausible enough; yet the fact is that few sights in this world are more depressing, and few experiences in this world more frustrating, than that of a group of students beating morosely away at the problem of self-understanding, spilling out on the common table the meager results of laborious introspection, using and pooling its joint insights on the problem of the self and coming out each day and each year precisely "at the same gate wherein it went." As Montaigne discovered once for all:

> 'Tis a rugged road, more so than it seems, to follow a pace so rambling and uncertain as that of the soul; to penetrate the dark profundities of its intricate internal windings; to choose and lay hold on so many little nimble notions."[3]

"The ego is more distant than any star."

The concern for the self and for a sure knowledge of the self is natural enough. The writer of Psalm 22:20 speaks of his soul as "my darling," and we know exactly what he means! Yet there *must* be something wrong with this procedure, this attempt to map by introspection the topography of the soul, this preoccupation with our own spiritual physiognomy. It seeks maturity by a procedure which is itself a sign of immaturity, and which is tolerable only in immaturity. At the superficial level at which it is generally conducted it is probably harmless enough, though it is a shocking waste of time; but it passes easily into a spiritual masturbation which is at best self-defeating, can be habit forming, and is at worst destructive of full humanity. The preliminary point that needs to be made here is that the measure of the self's maturity is its extrication from this pre-occupation with the self: it is not misleading to say that maturity may be measured by the degree to which we are bored with the self and with the self's problems. But try to put *that* point across in a contemporary student group—or, for that matter, in any group! The purpose of this writing will be served if, in the end, even a few people are persuaded to buy it.

THE MEASURE OF MAN

The self's concern to understand itself is legitimate and inevitable. But to pursue it solely by introspection is self-defeating. Some discoveries are to be made that way. They may in fact be very substantial discoveries: but the seductiveness of the introspective approach to the problems of the self derives in part from the fact that it feeds the self's preoccupation with the self, and in part from the fact that it lends itself to endless self-deception. No doubt the serpent that eats its own tail gets nourishment of a sort and for a time, but the procedure is subject to a law of diminishing returns. And so with the self or the soul. The more diligently the self is explored, the less of a self there is to explore. If a man were as an animal is, shut up like a fruit in its skin (a phrase of Martin Buber's), then the substance of the self might be explored from rind to core, its structure diagramed, its tex-

20

ture tested; but the very human capacity for introspection testifies to a dimension beyond this, a dimension which tends to be contracted as the self turns in upon itself. By its concern with itself the self destroys itself; this may be the very meaning of damnation.

> Hell is a place of everlasting noise,
> Where voices, plaintive and obnoxious, cry
> Over and over again their favorite word
> In constant iteration; I, I, I.

Further, introspection is an instrument which is far from uniformly effective from man to man. Some seem to be superbly skilled with it, though none, I think is free from the hazards of self-deception. Yet to some men there does seem to be given an extraordinary clarity of inward vision, the capacity to recover and to describe the detailed structure and functioning of the self, its interior life and its intimate modes and moods. Kierkegaard is a signal case; and even in our own prosaic day Thomas Merton, for example, can give you the most meticulous account of his mental and emotional states, not only today but day by day throughout his spiritual history: a detailed topography of the soul, a precise chart of its daily journey. Yet I hesitate to believe that anything crucial for human life, or for the kind of self-knowledge in which full human life consists, depends upon a capacity so unequally distributed, apparently according to temperament and even according to geographic and ethnic origin. I am peculiarly reluctant to believe that it depends upon a skill in which I am myself most notably inept. For the typical Lowland Scot, who I am bound to believe is not excluded from beatitude, is as free of imagination as he is of ulcers and, if he busied himself with introspection, would bring up from the hinterland of consciousness nothing better, I'm afraid, than a vague and non-committal blur.

Fortunately, the fact of the matter is that the procedure of introspection is only one among many which are both available and necessary if we are to seek and find the measure and the meaning of our humanity. To set them out in order may help to hold in focus and in proportion the real use and the real limits of introspection.

In the first place, we have to take seriously the insistence of the physical, biological, psychological, and social sciences that if you want the measure of man the first and most important thing to do—certainly the first thing, hypothetically the most important thing—is to *measure* him. If the structure of a man's life is in some sense a fixed and "given" thing; if, as Jesus says, a man cannot increase his stature by so much as one cubit, then it is important to take seriously the character of the "given," to estimate rightly what that stature is. And we have a growing battery of tools for precisely that kind of measurement. We are able with increasing exactness to diagram the structure and measure the dynamics of man—and that not only at the level of anatomy, physiology, and biology but also the psychic and social structures which are the business of psychology and sociology, the so-called "human sciences."

In view of the extraordinary gains which these disciplines go on making, it is imperative that two things be clear:

1) From any authentic Christian point of view, it is totally out of order to be negative or restrictive about the range and possibility of scientific work. There is no place at all in Christian thought for the so-called "gap theology," for any attempt to fence off some remote area of the cosmos, or some dark hinterland of the consciousness, from which science is

to be excluded in order that it may remain a happy hunting ground for pious speculation, a sort of toe hold for God. Insofar as the scientific method has its limits, they are limits which the scientist must draw for himself in terms of his own methods and their utility; no scientist worth his keep will accept restrictions put upon his work by what Tillich would call a "heteronomous" theology: that is, a theology which claims to qualify the legitimate autonomy of science, its right to do its own work in its own way. No theology may delimit the operation of science, define what method it shall use, or specify in advance of scientific inquiry what science will or will not find out. Of course, there may be situations in which for humane or Christian reasons the scientist may deny himself the use of certain procedures because the potential results are not worth the cost (*vivisection* has been the area of passionate debate); but here the point is not that certain kinds of knowledge may not be sought but that in this as in other lines of human endeavor the game must be worth the candle, the human gain must justify the human cost.

Scientific work is a positive activity whose charter, ultimately, is in the Christian doctrine of creation itself. A philosophy of the idealist type—or a piety of the Hindu-Buddhist type—which lives on a distinction between reality and appearance, will be negative or at best halfhearted about science because it concerns itself with appearance and not with ontological reality; but a Biblical doctrine, which knows nothing of such a distinction or which at least does not operate with it, which gives man "dominion over the earth," is a charter of scientific work and has been so historically. As John Baillie demonstrated concisely in his address before the British Association for the Advancement of Science,[4] the way was not clear for modern empirical and experimental science

23

until a decisive break was made with the classic and Greek notion of the world as a rationally intelligible emanation from the divine Reason, the details of whose parts could be arrived at by deduction from the rationally necessary character of the whole; and this break was made by the Christian affirmation that the world is not an emanation from divine and rational Mind, but the free creation of the divine Will brought into being out of nothing and established in its own proper and relative autonomy. From this point of view nothing can be known a priori about the structure of the world, since the mystery of the divine Will is hidden even from the most rational of men. The world, therefore, becomes the sphere of free exploration, in which the ways of God may be known to honest inquiry but are not susceptible to rational definition in advance of observation.

> . . . the conception of nature of the ancient Greek physicists, and indeed that of Aristotle, required to be profoundly dehumanized, desentimentalized: a rigorous mathematical determinism and soulless mechanism became the right and necessary ideal of physical science.[5]

This is the Roman Catholic philosopher-theologian Baron Von Hugel in his *The Mystical Element of Religion*, making essentially the same point which Baillie elaborated in his British Association lecture. The direct or indirect dependence of the scientific attitude upon the Christian doctrine of creation has become a commonplace even among those who do not make the Christian commitment of faith.

2) In the study of man, the knowledge that science gives us is substantial and not peripheral knowledge. We do not go along with the "orthodox" of whom the English poet and positivist Kathleen Nott complains in her vigorous as-

24

sault on the new piety called *The Emperor's Clothes.*[6] They insist, she says, that science can tell us nothing about men which it is really important to know.

> To say that test tubes and calipers not only never did, but never can, tell us anything direct about the Nature of Man (if we can for purposes of discussion accept that abstraction) is, even if true, not the same thing as saying that observation and the hypotheses based on observation cannot tell us anything about the subject.

As John Baillie says, "There is a natural history of the soul,"[7] that is to say, of the self.

> For man not only transcends nature but is a part of it. Nor is there any region of the soul's experience to the understanding of which scientific procedure has not its own contribution to make. There is a natural science of psychology. There is a natural science of sociology.

Man is, whatever else he is, "a very strange and special element in the cosmic-terrestrial, the physico-chemical, the organic-biotic processes of universal existence."[8]

In *Battle for the Mind*[9] William Sargant has a fascinating description of the biological and psychological concomitants of "religious" phenomena, especially of conversion. It would be wrongheaded for pious persons to resist a study of this kind.

Here are two illustrations of the legitimacy, and the legitimate autonomy, of scientific work, the first from anatomy, the second from psychology.

During World War II, with a clerical colleague, I conducted a mission in Trinity College, Dublin, that ancient university famous among many things for its medical school.

Early in the proceedings, we were mildly astonished to receive from a well-known professor of anatomy an invitation to take tea with him and then visit his dissecting room. We were puzzled only because the man was notorious for his outspoken atheism and did not normally seek out men of the cloth; but tea was always welcome and I for one had never seen a dissecting room. When we got among the cadavers, in various stages of dissection, it was clear that our medical friend assumed that the superstitions of religion could flourish only among men who were strangers to the facts of life—and death. His hope was that we would shake off our medieval hang-over if we could be induced to take seriously the anatomical structure which is all there is of man—at least on the dissecting table. His intention was entirely charitable. Actually we thought little of his argument, which had no particular originality about it—but we were bound to admire his work. Among other exhibits he showed us a series of wall plaques, which had been made, as far as I could understand the matter, as follows: He had taken a cadaver, injected into the organs certain colored fluids which apparently also helped to solidify it, and then sliced it into inch-thick sections which were displayed in orderly series, behind glass, around the walls of the lab. The effect was a series of plane sections showing the relative position of the organs at various "latitudes" of the human body. An invaluable device, as it seemed to me: revealing facts of life which were true apart from Christian dogma, were unaffected *by* Christian dogma, facts about which theology in a word had nothing to say, or at least nothing to say which would affect one way or another the validity of the data. Yet these were data on which theologians like other men might be crucially dependent, and the

26

surgeon himself was custodian of a knowledge which at its own level was vital to the human good.

There is also a valid and valuable anatomy of the psyche, which is the business of psychology. In my parish in New Zealand, there was a young married man who was making havoc of his home, in spite of every good intention, by unresolved psychological tensions which drove him alternately to church and to drink, though he was clearly incapable of winning any reassurance from either. We were out of reach of competent psychiatric help, so I tried the following: I spent two long evenings, far into the night, bullying and battering him to tell me the story of his life in full and with every seemingly irrelevant detail. Everything he told me I got down in some fashion; but the result, to me, was a hopeless jumble of facts and impressions about home relations, sex experience, and so on. To the pious amateur in psychology it made no sense at all. I made two copies. One I sent by air to a Christian psychotherapist in England, one to an atheist friend of mine, well trained in therapy, in New Zealand. Their diagnoses came back promptly, almost simultaneously—and they were identical. So positive were they that they said in effect: "You can take it from here." And so it was. The "patient" was provided, by the atheist as by the Christian, with such a precise understanding of his own problem, which had been beyond his reach and mine, that the healing process began then and has continued, lo, these many years, to a condition of psychological health and family stability.

It was clear that here, in the most intimate area of the self, was a set of hard, resistant data whose meaning was unillumined by piety, yet accessible to scientific work on condition not of piety but of competence.

Man *is* an element in the physicochemical, organic-biotic

27

process; he is also, as Marx put it, "the ensemble of the social relations"; and even if that is not all that he is, yet what he is cannot be fully or truly accounted for unless these levels are taken seriously and dealt with in their own terms. And they are not separate but related areas of investigation: I know a positivist philosopher who took successive years for the study of anatomy, psychology, and sociology because he believed that no valid account of man's "being" can afford to neglect his bone structure or anything else that is factually true about him. From the point of view of a Biblical faith which accepts the psychosomatic unity of man this is not necessarily heretical.

Science is an activity consonant with man's created nature, in which God-given gifts are utilized for the purpose for which they were given: and as such it generates its own virtues and honors God by its achievements, even when its practitioners are atheists and its conclusions in what Von Hugel calls "friction" with orthodoxy. Of course any scientist, no matter what his field, is subject to the normal human temptation to exalt his specialty and to exaggerate his achievement—but that is an indictment of human nature and not of science. Insofar as Christianity has a special problem with the scientist, it is not so much to teach him the limitations of his method (which could be a piece of impertinence) as to validate the dignity of his calling, and to remind him of his stature and his limitations as a man. For there is no doubt that scientific activity, like business activity, or war, or churchmanship, can so fill the horizon of those who practice it that the truth of life is distorted, and life itself is truncated. Darwin himself testified that his "higher tastes were atrophied" as his mind became "a kind of machine for grinding general laws out of large collections of facts."[10] David Riesman quotes a scientist's own affirmation that the claims of compassion must give way to the claims of science. It is from Claude Bernard's *An Introduction to the Study of Experimental Medicine:*

> A physiologist is not a man of fashion, he is a man of science, absorbed by the scientific idea he pursues; he no longer hears the cry of animals, he no longer sees the blood that flows, he sees only his idea and perceives only organisms concealing problems which he intends to solve.[11]

Darwin was rueful about the curtailment of humanity involved in scientific concentration. Bernard is not rueful, but evangelical, in his insistence that normal human considerations are to be sacrificed on the altar of scientific objectivity. This is the idolatry of science, and the man who gives way to it is eventually the man who with true scientific piety

> . . . would peep and botanize
> Upon his mother's grave.

Our university labs, fortunately from the human point of view, are fairly free of this inordinate worship of the scientific method. Most of our scientific workers are content to do an honorable job on the basis of a reasonable, even a Christian, conviction of its real but relative importance. Yet even where there is not the dogmatism of scientism, there can be an implicit absolutization of the habits of science to the point of an incapacity to handle those areas of life in which scientific objectivity is out of place. There are too many scientific workers of high competence who are babes-in-arms outside the laboratory. One of the leading biologists of this country took occasion to point out to his professional colleagues at a recent congress that their marital records are as bad as those of any group in the community; and I know of one scientist of standing who, when his wife protested his proposal to break up a long marriage, responded with this masterpiece of fatuity, "But surely we can be objective about this!" This inanity and lack of human sensitivity can be and often is the dire end result of that truncated vision of which Darwin had the good sense to be wary. Objectivity is a valid and valuable discipline for certain legitimate but limited and subordinate human ends: it is not a form of *pietas* to which human life is to be sacrificed. H. Richard Niebuhr points out that

> A scientist choosing his vocation or promising to love and cherish a life-partner cannot act on the hypothesis that there is no consciousness of self and no self but only an impersonal process of mind and matter.[12]

It is to this non-objective level of life that John Baillie points when having said that there is a natural science of psychology ("a natural history of the soul") he goes on to say, "there is also a knowledge of the psyche which is not a natural science at all."

> Natural science knows its objects only from without, having no insight into the inward secrets of their behavior. . . . But the secret of our behavior is known to us also from within.[13]

And that brings us in proper order to the second mode of apprehension of the self. To the valid deliverances of measurement we add the way of *introspection*, not in order to say to the objective observer "thus far and no farther," but simply because there is no reason in the world why we should not look at the self from any angle from which it looks interesting. Karl Heim, in *Christian Faith and Natural Science*, discriminates measurement and introspection in terms which are worth quoting:

> I can look at my body from outside. I can look at it in the mirror, in order to have the view of it which other people receive who look at it from without. If I happen to be a doctor or a scientist myself, I can examine parts of my body anatomically. I can carry out a blood test and subject the specimen to chemical analysis. I can X-ray my lung and so arrive at the most exact possible diagnosis. In all this I am always concerned with forming an "outside picture". . . . But this forming an "outside picture" of me reaches a quite definite limit at which the competence of my fellow human beings ceases, no matter how earnestly they may strive to advance further. There is an innermost area to which I myself alone have direct access, and into which nobody else can look.[14]

Heim might have added that the work of psychological science is subject to the same limitations in principle which he here attaches to anatomy and physiology: it too provides an invaluable "outside picture," and it is free to fill in as many details of the picture as it can discern, but it is still "outside."

Notice that the objective and introspective do not refer to two discrete areas of investigation. They deal with the same *self*, but from differing points of view; and there is a curious overlapping in that, for example, a deceptive self-awareness may be saved from illusion by rigorous psychoanalysis. Put more simply, the human sciences can save us from kidding ourselves about what we think we discover by introspection.

Montaigne, that master of common sense, knew very well what is at stake here:

> . . . into how many parts have they divided the soul? . . . they have the power granted them to rip, place, displace, piece and stuff it, every one according to his own fancy, and yet to this day they possess it not.[15]

It seems unarguable that, as Montaigne goes on to say, "We are nearer neighbours to ourselves than the whiteness of snow or the weight of stones are to us: if a man does not know himself, how should he know his functions and powers?"

Yet there are many among the human scientists who maintain not only that the deliverances of introspection are subject to error and are assisted by analysis, which is true, but that the deliverances of introspection have no status at all, that consciousness is an epiphenomenon of the glandular, nervous, and muscular process, and that man's incorrigible consciousness of self-consciousness, freedom, and responsibility is illusory. Joseph Wood Krutch's book *The Measure of Man*[16] is a sustained assault upon the claim, which he finds widespread, that man's nature may be progressively known and "his thoughts controlled with precision," both by the application of the scientific method. Krutch's passionate protest is worth reading as the eloquent voice of the old-line humanism. We shall refer to it again. The point now is simply that in addition to the legitimate claims of measurement, introspection too has its place, and its deliverances their claim to attention. But to include the deliverances of introspection certainly does nothing to simplify our problem.

Man is a complex, burdened and pitiful creature. He may be the paragon of animals, of noble reason and of infinite faculty; in action he may be like an angel and in apprehension like a god; but he is also a petulant thinking reed and a hopeless mess. He is in love with life and also hates it deeply and subtly. He is capable of crime and sin but also has a tyrannical and whimsical conscience that tortures him for trivial misdemeanors as brutally as it punishes him for unpardonable sins. Narcissistic, he hates himself; full of insufferable vanity, he seeks to humiliate himself; the victim of systematic self-deception, he is capable of unsparing self-knowledge . . . it would take an Augustine, a Freud, a Dostoevsky, a Kierkegaard and a Shakespeare, aided by a Boas and a Machiavelli, pooling their several talents and techniques, to split open the secret heart of this contemptible lump of clay and extract its wonderful essence.[17]

Small wonder that the student bull session struggling for self-awareness is reduced to morose discouragement.

It would be simpler to believe that man is a complex machine, subject to measure and susceptible of control. Simpler, yes; but truer? "I have seen no such monster, or more express wonder of the world," said Montaigne, "than myself."

It is not our present business to attempt to elucidate the content of introspection, or even to illustrate the kind of discoveries men claim to have made about themselves as they prowl through the recesses of the interior life. Most of us, I suspect, would go along with Krutch in considering man's incorrigible conviction of freedom and responsibility to be a primary brute datum, as firm as the deliverances of

33

the physical sciences: a primary datum to which the determinist scientist himself pays tribute when he claims the *right* to do his own work in his own way; to which the materialist Bentham paid unconscious homage when he declared that the word "ought" *ought* to be banished from the dictionary; to which Marx witnesses when he rages against the *wrong* done to man by the tyranny of the bourgeois notions of right and wrong.

But the confidence we place in introspection ought to be a moderated confidence. For its deliverances are conditioned not only by innate capacity or lack of it but by neurotic and organic factors of all kinds. It is right to use it, and right to be wary of it. Then again, even those who set store by it and seem to use it with facility are by no means unanimous in their reports. Not all of us come up from the exploration of the inner reaches of the self with Kierkegaard's unambiguous conviction of "our responsibility to the Other, who transcends our self-consciousness and yet is known in our self-consciousness." This may be because we have not, in Kierkegaard's phrase, "plumbed our self-consciousness to the depths"; but on the other hand it looks as if equally devoted explorers of the *psyche* come with equal conviction to a belief in man's wretchedness and in his responsible dignity— we have to set Sartre, for example, with Kierkegaard.

Add introspection to measurement and we still have to say with Karl Jaspers:

The very fact that we do not know what man really is, is an essential part of our humanity.[18]

THE LOCATION OF MAN

Much can be learned by observation, even common sense observation unaided by instruments. I saw a prominent athlete at Stanford walk into a post the other day as he took observations of a fetching coed, and no doubt he was gathering valid statistical data. And when the data of observation is refined by laboratory techniques the volume and importance of the information so gathered is, as we have seen, substantial. But it is still statistical. It is limited not by any enforced proscription, but by the stubborn insistence of the self that its interior knowledge of itself be taken seriously and added to the data of measurement. Introspection is valid and illuminating, but it is difficult and deceptive, and its data impossible to tabulate.

Of these two approaches to the knowledge of the self it is important to mark the use and limits. But as a matter of homely fact for our identification of ourselves, our estimate and measure of ourselves, we depend normally on neither of them. Notice a few vulgar human facts. If I ask you who you are, you do not reply either with statistics (the data of measurement) *or* with the data of introspection. You do not say, "I am a five-foot-ten-inch, one-hundred-and-seventy-pound introvert with a tendency to anxiety neurosis." You may not even give me your name, first of all, but if you do give me your name, it consists of a surname and a "given" name, both of which identify you not by reference to your physical and psychic constitution, but by your relation to your immediate family (normally) and to your ancestral line. Usually, however, you will say something like, "I am a Harvard sophomore, majoring in politics, the son of So-and-so, who is a farm foods dealer in Kewanee, Illinois." In other

35

words, you identify yourself by *locating* yourself, in a family and in a community. This ordinary human instinct to define the self by its relationships is of the utmost importance. We shall consider what it means, in a more sophisticated way, in a moment. But it is not simply the result of reticence about the interior life. As I know you better I shall no doubt learn more about your interior life; but it is my profound conviction that all that I may learn about it, even in the most intimate confidences, will be less coherent, less cogent, and less vital for the understanding of what really makes you tick than that set of relationships which you instinctively reeled off at our first meeting when I asked you who you were. Even the questions children ask about themselves, *pace* Paul Tillich, have less to do with psychic and ontological structure than they have to do with relationships. Tillich at the age of six may have been preoccupied with questions like "Why is there not nothing?" "Why am I part of the totality of Being?"—but I beg leave to doubt it. I think that that is the product of Tillich's reflective hindsight. In any event, apart from Tillich, I have yet to learn of a child pulling petals off daisies while chanting "Being, Not-Being, Being, Not-Being. . . ." The more usual formula is "She loves me. She loves me not. She loves me. . . ." For at that stage and at every stage *that* is what matters, not our status in Being but our status in Love. It is only a somewhat fevered sophomoric imagination that would say, "In the timelessness of the history of all men's lives, a great agonizing cry arises: 'Who am I?' " The authentic human questions are not cries in the void but questions generated out of human, which is to say social, experience. "Will I make the team?" "Will I make the grade?" "Will I win the girl?" "How can you ever forgive

36

me?" They are questions not about the self's Being, but about the self's *status*.

For true knowledge and real identification, it is not sufficient that the self be *dissected*, either anatomically or psychically; it also must be *located*. This is, I take it, in colloquial terms, what Martin Buber has been insisting on since the publication of his *I and Thou* back in 1937.[19] He recently put the matter as follows, in an address to a gathering of psychiatrists in Washington, D.C.:

> The animal is like the fruit in its skin . . . while man is in the world as a dweller in an enormous building which is always being added to, and to whose limits he can never penetrate. . . .
> The human person needs confirmation. . . . An animal does not need it. In man, the innermost growth of the self is not unfolded in his relationship to himself, but between him and others. . . . This is the mutuality of the making present, the mutuality of acceptance and affirmation. This confirmation can come only from one human being to another.[20]

Man knows himself *as* a self, and knows what it means to *be* a self, only in relation to other selves which confront him in equal freedom and selfhood. Man is anatomic, biologic, psychic, ontological—but the meaning of his existence is, in Buber's word, *dialogic*. He cannot know who he is until he is *told* who he is. Just as a man can have no more than the vaguest adumbration of what sex means outside of sex relations, so he can have no better than the vaguest idea of what personality means outside of personal relations.[21] A man knows himself as he is known by another; and, since it

37

is love that opens the one to the other, then the greater the love the greater the knowledge.

It is this actual and potential "openness" of man (what Niebuhr calls his "self-transcendence") which defines a further way of approach to the self beyond those of measurement and introspection. Karl Jaspers puts it clearly:

> All other living beings are at once confined and consummated in their peculiar structure, but man is boundlessly open. . . .[22]
>
> In contradistinction to all the higher animals, man acquires his specific life-form "in the open," in a free and rich relationship to living creatures, and, above all, to other human beings.[23]

Since this is so, his life can have no definition, no form, except as it is shaped, defined, and in some sense limited by its encounters with other selves.

Neither measurement nor introspection can possibly, in the nature of the case, give us a firm estimate of the worth of a man, or of *this* man. And actually our estimate of our own worth is wrought less out of measurement, or introspection, than it is out of the communities of our nurture and the encounters in which we are caught. Watch the man who has an average "guid conceit o' himsel' " revise his whole estimate of himself at the moment he falls in love. You can see it on campus. The Stanford or Harvard man who is, as touching the fraternity law, blameless, knows himself for the skunk he is just as soon as he is made captive to love; and the better the girl and the more he is loved the more radical the revision he makes of his own estimate of himself. "A man is known by the company he keeps." But it is also true that a man knows *himself* by the company he keeps. We all know people of whom we say, "He makes me feel like a louse" and others of whom we say, "He makes me feel ten feet tall." In his introduction to Charles Williams' *The Descent of the Dove*[24] W. H. Auden says of Williams:

> I have met great and good men in whose presence one was conscious of one's own littleness; Charles Williams' effect on me and on others with whom I have spoken was quite different: in his company one felt twice as intelligent and infinitely nicer than, out of it, one knew oneself to be.

Notice that this revelatory self-awareness which is generated out of personal encounter depends upon the intensity of the encounter. For example, in J. D. Salinger's 1957 *New Yorker* story "Zooey"—a tour de force even for Salinger—Zooey comes to progressive self-knowledge out of the intensity of his compassionate wrestling with the problems of his neurotic sister. To yell with the crowd at the football game provides exhilaration but no particular illumination; there you really do "come out by the same gate wherein you went." But to work at the bench or on the barricades, to wage any kind of war, hot, cold, political, or Holy, in close comradeship and under heavy pressure—it is so that men in some sense "find themselves" and learn to some degree to measure "the stature of the soul."

This is a subtle business, and the ramifications of it are explored in the writings of Buber and Niebuhr much more fully than we are able to do it here. Enough for now if it is clear that for the knowledge of the self it is not sufficient to *dissect* it; it is necessary to *locate* it. It is *more* necessary to locate it, in point of fact, for it cannot at all be agreed that true self-knowledge is denied to those who have no skill in

psychic surgery. Even the problems which call for psychological healing are normally produced not by internal dislocation
calling for manipulation (though there is real need for devoted and skillful psychic surgery) but by broken relationships calling for reconciliation.

Man knows himself only in the presence of the other; but
the range of the inquiry into the structure and meaning of
selfhood has to be extended yet one stage further, even in
secular terms. For man is in daily dealings not only with
his immediate neighbors but with the family of mankind insofar as its common life and its common inheritance im-
pinge upon *his* life. It is commonplace that Western thought
tends in general, as it is idealist or naturalist, to identify the
humanum of man, his essential humanness, either with the
mind or with the organism. But if we are to give proper
weight to all that has been said so far we shall have to say,
rather, that *man is his history:* and this must include, certainly, his physiological, biological, and psychological history; but also and perhaps chiefly his social history, his
profound involvement in that community of nurture which
is the matrix in which his life is set. While Western thought
has been dominated by the somewhat barren debate between
idealism and naturalism, this emphasis has recurred, for example in Vico and, more immediately, in R. G. Collingwood.
In Collingwood it is in too close affinity with idealism, with
an excessive emphasis upon conscious and rational elements
in life and history, but what he has to say is none the less to
the present point:

Man, who desires to know everything, desires to know
himself. . . . Without some knowledge of himself, his

knowledge of other things is imperfect. . . . Self-knowledge, here, means not knowledge of man's bodily nature, his anatomy and physiology; nor even a knowledge of his mind, so far as that consists of feeling, sensation and emotion; but a knowledge of his knowing faculties, his thought or understanding or reason. . . .

Such knowledge, according to Collingwood, was sought by Locke, Kant, and Hume, among others, by an approach based on the analogy of the natural sciences. Modern psychology proposes the same undertaking with improved techniques. For Collingwood the enterprise is misconceived: "the 'science of human nature' broke down because its method was distorted by analogy with the natural sciences."

. . . the right way of investigating nature is by the methods called scientific, the right way of investigating minds is by the methods of history . . . the work which was to be done by the science of human nature is actually done, and can only be done, by history.[25]

There is a nice question of definition here, especially about the meaning of "mind"; earlier in the book he puts the matter in terms more like those I have been using.

What is history "for"? . . . History is "for" human self-knowledge. It is generally thought to be of importance to man that he should know himself: where knowing himself means knowing not merely his personal characteristics, but his nature as man. Knowing yourself means knowing, first, what it means to be a man; secondly, knowing what it means to be the kind of man you are; and thirdly, knowing what it is to be the man *you* are and nobody else is. Knowing yourself means knowing what you can do; and since nobody knows what he can do until he tries, the only clue to what man can do is what man has done. The value of history, then, is that it teaches us what man has done and thus what man is.[26]

This may be too absolute, but in an age and a generation overmuch given to introspection it helps to keep the balance. J. V. Langmead Casserley puts it more precisely:

> Personal life is lived, of necessity, in history and in self-conscious depth at the same time. The historian who has not made the existential discovery of the impenetrable depths of the human consciousness . . . cannot appreciate the kind of being it is his function to be historical about. But if the non-existentialist historian cannot identify the person, the non-historical existentialist cannot locate him.[27]

For the balance of this discussion our problem is to get ourselves located.

NOTES TO CHAPTER I

1. *Orthodoxy*. Dodd, Mead & Company, Inc., New York, 1952, pp. 96–97.
2. Morris, Charles: *The Christian Century*, July 24, 1957.
3. Montaigne: Essays. Quoted Santillana. *The Age of Adventure*. Mentor Books, 1956, p. 171.
4. Baillie, John: *Natural Science and the Spiritual Life*. Charles Scribner's Sons, New York, 1952.
5. Baillie: *op. cit.*, p. 34.
6. Nott, Kathleen: *The Emperor's Clothes*. William Heinemann Ltd., London, 1953. (The book is a lively assault on the

fashionable apologetics. She has respect for but small confidence in T. S. Eliot, she is ironic about Dorothy Sayers, and she has a profound distaste for and distrust in C. S. Lewis. In an overpious age it is very refreshing.)

7. Baillie: *op. cit.*, p. 40.

8. Barth, Karl: *Against the Stream.* SCM Press, London, 1954, p. 187.

9. Sargant, William: *Battle for the Mind.* Doubleday & Company, Inc., New York, 1957.

10. Baillie: *op. cit.*, pp. 8–9. Darwin, F: *Life and Letters of Charles Darwin.* Vol. I, pp. 100ff, 304ff.

11. Bernard, Claude: *An Introduction to the Study of Experimental Medicine.* Quoted, Riesman, David: *The Lonely Crowd.* Doubleday Anchor Book, 1956, p. 290.

12. Niebuhr, H. Richard: *The Meaning of Revelation.* The Macmillan Company, New York, 1946, p. 105.

13. Baillie: *op. cit.*, p. 41.

14. Heim, Karl: *Christian Faith and Natural Science.* Harper & Brothers, New York, 1957, p. 84.

15. Montaigne Quoted Santillana *op. cit.*, p. 185.

16. Krutch, Joseph Wood: *The Measure of Man.* Bobbs-Merrill Company, Indianapolis, 1953.

17. Vivas: *The Moral Life and the Ethical Life.* University of Chicago Press, Chicago, 1950, p. 60.

18. Jaspers, Karl: *The Origin and Goal of History.* Yale University Press, New Haven, 1953, p. 35.

19. Buber, Martin: *I and Thou.* Translated by Ronald Gregor-Smith. Edinburgh. T. and T. Clark, Edinburgh, 1937. Buber's crucial argument is given varied and readable expression in J. H. Oldham's *Life is Commitment* (SCM Press, London, 1953), and is developed in an original and comprehensive fashion in Reinhold Niebuhr's *The Self and the Dramas of History* (Charles Scribner's Sons, New York, 1955).

20. Buber, Martin: Address given April 1, 1957.

21. It is not without meaning that the Biblical word for sexual intercourse means, and is in English translated to mean, *knowledge*, e.g., Genesis 4:1: "And Adam *knew* Eve his wife, and she conceived. . . ."

43

22. Jaspers: *op. cit.*, p. 47.
23. *Ibid.*, p. 38.
24. Williams, Charles: *The Descent of the Dove.* Living Age Books, New York, 1956. (The book itself, which we shall refer to again, is possibly the finest church history in English—certainly it is one of the finest.)
25. Collingwood, R. G. *The Idea of History.* Clarendon Press, Oxford, 1946, pp. 205-9.
26. *Ibid.*, p. 10.
27. Casserley, J. V. Langmead: *The Christian in Philosophy.* Faber & Faber, Ltd., London, 1949, p. 224.

CHAPTER II

The Mirror of History

We are in history as a fish is in water. . . .
H. RICHARD NIEBUHR[1]

I have mixed my metaphors before the chapter is well begun: but the trouble is that no single simile does justice to that dimension of life and of man with which I now want to deal.

If we agree to work a while with the notion that *man is his history*, then we accept it as including physiological, genetic, psychological history, and so on. The cruciality of this dimension of life is being forced on our attention in these present days. We have learned to accept the fact that the character of a man may be profoundly disturbed or distorted by "natural" factors—by psychological storms beating up out of the unconscious, or by genetic damage falling out of the clouds. This is true, it is immeasurably important, and it is deeply disquieting. Nonetheless, insofar as we are left with a human life to live, that life is also profoundly conditioned by social and cultural history; and an understanding of what it means

45

to live a human life involves a serious grappling with our cultural heritage.

I begin by paraphrasing part of an eloquent argument by that notable philosopher of science, Max Otto, in his *Science and the Moral Life*.[2] He refers to a book of moral counsel, published about a century ago, which offered "a very simple method which, if followed, will lead youth from confusion and doubt to clearness and certainty." Simply stated, the "method" was to abandon confidence in one's own judgment and put one's trust in "properly constituted authorities;" specifically, in parents, civil rulers, and the clergy. These divinely appointed authorities together constitute a repository of ancient wisdom which we should not oppose with our own confused and precarious notions of right and wrong. By deferring to them, we "are sure to obtain the wisdom and strength necessary for living life at its highest and fullest." Otto then says:

How much of an appeal a book of this kind was able to make when it was published . . . I have no way of telling. But I know, and so do you, how much of an appeal it would make to thoughtful youths today. It would make none.

And he goes on to argue that in fact all three authorities are suspect, and in principle they must be ineffectual because the present generation has been introduced to a world profoundly different, and to problems utterly diverse, from any which our forebears knew:

. . . it may be questioned whether there has ever before been so widespread, so sophisticated, so confident a challenge of the older by the younger generation.

46

That was written in 1949. I'm not sure that even then the younger generation was as confident of its power to stand on its own two feet as Otto suggests (my guess is that he is still thinking of 1929); but I am certain that as far as 1957 goes he is way off the mark. There is, indeed, a very general feeling that the wisdom of the elders has not carried us very far or left us a very cheerful world. I admit also that few undergraduates of my acquaintance are very consciously indebted to the church on the corner; but they didn't give it up because it was too authoritative or too confident of its own divine prerogatives, but because it had nothing particular to say. And they don't exchange the church's authority for their own sure moral insights, but only to huddle fearfully in another "crowd." Within my own recent experience I heard two baccalaureate sermons, by prominent ecclesiastics who ought to have known better, which exhorted the assembled graduates to "stand on their own two feet," "stand up and be counted," and so on; all of which I found profoundly unimpressive, since a score of those very graduates had earlier passed through my office, confessing that they shook at the knees at the very thought of graduating. They had never in their lives stood up to be counted, had toed timidly the fraternity line (shouting raucously the while to keep their spirits up), and had no confidence at all in their capacity to stand on their own two feet.

I think that we can detect, actually, the beginning at least of a trend contrary to that which Otto imagines—nothing so dramatic as a new deference to parents and the clergy, but a number of symptoms which add up to something which may not misleadingly be called, and sometimes is called, a "new conservatism." In religion for example there is an extraordinary appeal in authoritarian piety of the most diverse

47

kinds, be it the ancient wisdom of the Roman *magisterium*, or the simple "The Bible says. . . ." of Billy Graham; in politics there is no need to emphasize, especially at Harvard, the appeal of the New Conservatism officially so called; and one may take the resurgence of interest in curricular and extracurricular religious activity to mean in part a conviction that if we are to improve upon our inheritance we ought to begin by understanding it. In sexual mores too: one of our leading journals ran an article recently on what it called "The New Monogamy," a certain revulsion from sexual rebellion and a feeling after the values of stability and fidelity, a return in this matter also to the traditions of the fathers.

I am not contending that this is unqualifiedly good. I shall argue later, for example, that the New Conservatism in politics is a very mixed blessing indeed. I think, however, that it is all too slick to dismiss it as a mere hankering for authority; it is in part certainly a revulsion from a life which is intellectually and morally *shapeless*. In any event it does mean that we have a reasonably good chance of a hearing when we plead that history and tradition be taken seriously, as a vital and not an antiquarian interest.

And that is what I now propose to do, but in a particular sense and for a specific purpose. It is an important fact of the contemporary intellectual situation that the theology and philosophy of history is being studied with renewed eagerness, and that Christian thinkers are among the most influential participants in the discussion.[3] Reasons for this are implied in the two following chapters. But this is not our subject. Nor am I proposing a capsule history of culture, or even of Western culture. That would be a piece of nonsense in the space we have. Karl Marx it was who said that to be a good Communist one must make one's own the whole of philosophy; one must pass it, as it were, through one's own contemporary mind, for only the man who has a mastery of philosophy has the right to debunk it. The challenge is salutary, but our intention is more modest.

There is in fact a good deal of history, even of intellectual history, which we can afford to forget. I heard one of our better local disc jockeys tell the story of a certain ship's captain, who spent forty years of honorable service at sea. He was held in respect and affection by all who worked with him. Only one thing puzzled them. It was observed that each morning, before he went on the bridge, he opened a locked desk in his cabin, removed a sheet of paper, read it, returned it, and locked the desk again. So he served his forty years, and he died. His associates buried him decently—and then made a dive for the desk to see what was on the mysterious paper. It read simply: "The *left* side is the port side." There are some things we can afford to forget: we can always look them up. And this applies also to the vast agglomeration of fact and event, of proposition and counterproposition, of movement and debate, which constitutes general history and cultural history.

Nonetheless, while the vast panorama is beyond our intellectual vision, while some parts of it are blurred by distance, certain elements of our cultural history are utterly necessary to our understanding of ourselves. We noticed in the previous chapter that we tend instinctively to identify ourselves not by reference to the internal structure of the self, but by reference to our ancestry and to the community of our nurture. The instinct is a sound one; for our rational and moral life is largely constituted from elements in our inheritance, and without some knowledge of that inheritance *we are unintelligible to ourselves.*

One of the things that puzzles the undergraduate who is trying to make sense of his life, especially of his moral life, is that he is held by certain convictions and guided by certain "instincts" of approval or repulsion, which he would find very difficult to defend, rationally, either to himself or to other people. And this worries him, because he belongs in a tradition which pays deep deference to reason. Yet the same tradition has built into his make-up elements of conviction and devotion which lie much deeper than formal logic. The fact is that to understand the structure of our moral life, "what makes us tick," our built-in mechanisms of moral attraction and repulsion, it is necessary to refer in the first instance to history rather than to reason. Let me give two illustrations of particular interest to me as an exiled Scot.

When I go back periodically to the Western Isles or, for that matter, to Glasgow, I am impressed again and again with the fact that I am in the presence of a tradition of behavior which has roots that lie far below rational explanation. It's an odd and a mixed tradition: There is, for example, a stubbornness and intransigence in the Highlander which can work both good and harm; he can be as stiff-necked in a private feud as he has been in the face of tyrants. But for weal or woe his stubbornness is inexplicable, whatever else goes into it, without reference to the tradition of faith and morals which goes back specifically to John Knox. And the strange strain of gentility, which affects the Glasgow tram conductor and infects with grace even a public transport system, has roots at least as deep. It means, for example, that the sorely tried worker among the Glasgow "gangs" who make a habit of wielding bicycle chains and make great play with razor blades has at least something to appeal to, a certain "tradition of civility" (to use a phrase which Walter

50

Lippmann has made current) which redeems the situation from utter hopelessness.

The chaplain of my own university told me of an experience which illustrates the same point. Needing some work done in his office, a job calling for specially skilled carpentry, he stated his needs to the university yard. They sent over a Scottish carpenter of dour countenance and solemn manner, with a jaw like the Rock of Gibraltar (how many a good and bad cause has been wrecked on that jaw!). He took his instructions, set to work, and finished the job with never a word. The work was difficult and intricate, but done so skillfully that when it was over the chaplain felt that some special commendation was called for. So in a few well-chosen words he spoke of his appreciation for a job well done. The craftsman turned, looked him straight in the eye, and spoke the only words he uttered during the whole transaction: "Whit did ye expec'?" said he. A tradition of craftsmanship which takes it for granted that work worth doing is worth doing well, which an older generation would have "explained" by saying something like "Holiness unto the Lord"—it takes centuries to develop it and, thank God, centuries to outgrow it. It cannot be taught, in the ordinary sense; it must be bred in the bone by generations of nurture. And many of us who are puzzled by our remnant integrity and our rationally inexplicable impulses to virtue are actually the beneficiaries of such a tradition.

It is not really strange that our convictions are normally stronger than the *reasons* we can give for them, for man is not reason simply, but *history*; and it is out of our history that our deep dispositions are generated, from a level far deeper than reason and logic. The odd thing is that we are restive about our "good" impulses—to thorough workmanship, to sexual restraint, to elementary honesty—because we cannot set them firm on rational and logical ground; and that too, as we have seen, is the legacy of a tradition which has strong rationalist elements in it, such that it is suspicious of convictions which either fall short of or run beyond rational explanation and justification. ✔

We are inexplicable to ourselves without reference to our history: and this is true both of our individual and of our social life. If I want to know what makes me tick morally, I shall find more illumination from a study of the Puritans than from the most diligent discipline of introspection. And the character of American society is similarly inexplicable without proper attention to the rock from which it was hewn. That's not a bad sentence, but it is a bit misleading; for a society as complex as this one is hewn not from one rock, even Plymouth Rock, but is a combination of many elements —it is Greek, it is Roman, it is Puritan, but it is much else as well. The American man is Homo Classicus, Homo Christianus, Homo Hebraicus, l'homme bourgeois—and he is also a frontiersman, a migrant, and a rebel. But though his make-up is as complex as his history, that is no reason why he should surrender his only chance of understanding it, which is to try to make sense of at least the salient elements of his inheritance.

I conducted a debate one time with a prominent philosopher of education, of an experimentalist stamp. (Notice as I tell the story that one of the fruits of original sin is that, in retrospect, one always wins and never loses a debate!) In my recollection, at any rate, it went like this: He maintained that when a teacher meets a class at the beginning of a school day there is a sort of *tabula rasa*, a totally "open" situation. It is a pure learning situation in which anything may happen;

the whole thing is unpredictable, dependent only on the dynamic dealing between teacher and pupil, between pupil and pupil, and between the whole learning community and the problems thrown up by their life together during the day. No presuppositions, no domination by tradition, a pure experiment in learning. So I asked, fairly obviously, what was the first thing the class did when they got together: "Salute the Flag," said he. "I pledge my allegiance to the Flag of the United States of America and to the Republic for which it stands. . . ." In other words, the whole enterprise is in fact set firmly within a tradition; it is ridden by presuppositions which can be well handled only if they are understood for what they are. And the work of education is revealed for what it actually is: not a free experiment in learning (though the experimentalists talk a lot of pedagogic sense along with their nonsense) but the transmission of a cherished tribal lore, the initiation of the young of the community into the best tradition of tribal wisdom.

As we shall see, this inextricable involvement of our individual and social life in the matrix of history and culture has its dangers and needs to be corrected and supplemented; but it is in the first place something for which to be devoutly thankful, as for the gift of life itself. For without it there is no life which is fully, or even approximately, human.

THE USES OF THE PAST

John Dewey is reported to have told a seminar at Columbia, "I have learned to take all my troubles back to Plato." It is perhaps odd that the famous pragmatist should choose Plato, and there can be more than one view of the hopefulness of this particular procedure; but there is no doubt that a familiarity with the great tradition is a resource for contemporary living. It gives us a stance of at least partial independence from the pressures of the time. It gives us membership in what G. K. Chesterton called "the democracy of the dead."

> Tradition is the democracy of the dead. Tradition refuses to submit to the small and arrogant oligarchy of those who simply happen to be walking about.[4]

When we are sensible of our community in vital faith and life with those who have shaped our inheritance and given us the values that we live by, it becomes more important to keep company with the great than to keep up with the Joneses. Reinhold Niebuhr says that

> . . . consistently "liberal" or "bourgeois" notions of conscience as purely individual do not do justice to the fact that the individual is best able to defy a community when his conscience is informed and reinforced by another community, whether religious or political. Perhaps the final paradox of the social and individual dimension of the moral life is revealed by the fact that the individual may defy a community which directly impinges upon his life and threatens his liberty by its coercions; but his defiance is usually undertaken in the name of another, more inclusive or more worthy community, even though that community makes no overt claims upon him and may exist only in his imagination.[5]

This may degenerate into romanticism of the baser sort; but surely it is true that the recollection of Thomas More on his way to the rickety scaffold:

> I pray you, Mr. Lieutenant, see me safe up; and for my coming down, let me shift for myself.

54

does tend to breed in us at least the aspiration after a like non-chalance in the face of death; and the conduct of Giordano Bruno on the pyre introduces us to a world of spaciousness and honor in which the conventions of this time and place press less sorely. And one does not need to be a Christian (after all, Bruno was a great deal less orthodox than More, but died as bravely) to relish More's response to the threat of penury in exchange for principle:

It shall not be best for us (he told his family) to fall to the lowest fare first. We will begin with Lincoln's Inn diet—then will we, if need be, the next year after go one step down to New Inn fare, wherewith many an honest man is well contented. If that exceed our ability, too, then will we the next year after descend to Oxford fare, where many grave, ancient and learned Fathers be conversant continually, which if our ability stretch not to maintain neither, then may we yet with bags and wallets go a-begging together, and hoping that for pity some good folks will give their charity at every man's door to sing *salve Regina*, and so keep company merrily together.[6]

There was some discussion in the ancient world as to whether the study of history helps men to avoid the mistakes of their predecessors, or simply gives them strength to endure the changes and chances of life with a courage learned from the culture heroes. Collingwood thinks that with the disappearance of the city-state men's confidence in their capacity to manage history was dissipated, so that Polybius, for example,

. . . does not think that the study of history will enable men to avoid the mistakes of their predecessors and surpass them in worldly success; the success to which the

55

study of history can lead is for him an inner success, a victory not over circumstances but over self.[7]

We have probably enough remnant confidence to believe that the study of history may give us some power to manipulate history as well as to endure it. Be that as it may, an immersion in the heroic tradition gives us at the least some high exhilaration in the company of the men of faith, even if their faith is not always our own.

But there is much more to be learned, especially about ourselves, from our specific inheritance; and to identify ourselves we have to identify that inheritance. Even if we can recover from the whole historic record no more than what Gordon Rupp calls "baskets of fragments,"[8] yet what we have is full of nourishment and of resources for the understanding of the self.

> . . . the substance of history consists in the experiences in which man gains the understanding of his humanity and together with it the understanding of his limits.[9]

What is for us this "substance of history"?

> [The substance of] history is that section of the past which, at any time, is clearly visible to man; it is the sector of things past which he can make his own, it is the consciousness of origins.[10]

This project of locating our "origins" is difficult enough, but at least it is more modest and more manageable than a comprehensive "interpretation of history." It was Bernard Lord Manning who said somewhere that if anyone begins a sentence with the phrase "All history teaches. . . ." you can bet that he is about to tell you a whopping lie. (This is no doubt rough on Toynbee, Hegel, Marx, Spengler, et al;

but since they tend to affirm with approximately equal confidence that "all history teaches" substantially different things, it would seem that Manning may have the right of it after all.) Our project is less hazardous, but it is risky enough. It is to ask what is that history without which we are inexplicable to ourselves: in what historic mirror are we to know ourselves for the kind of men we are?

THE HERITAGE OF THE WEST

In *The Origin and Goal of History*, Karl Jaspers produces a schema of world history which is less vulnerable than most such patterns if only because it is more general. At least it offers a suggestion of the way in which the history of the West may be, and indeed must be, distinguished from the general history of mankind. The general history of mankind, he maintains, comprises *four stages* in *three areas*: outside these three areas is the penumbra of continuing primitivism. The three significant areas are the *Orient-Occident* (by which he means the communities circling the Mediterranean and the cultures conditioned by them), *India*, and *China*. The Orient-Occident (the *West*) of course has colonial offshoots, for example, in Latin America and in Africa. As mankind emerges from *prehistory* (the first stage), we have the *Ancient Civilizations* (second stage) of Mesopotamia-Egypt, the Indus, and the Hwang Ho. While the development in time is not uniform, these civilizations are present in their integrity by the end of the third millennium B.C. And from that time on nothing truly novel emerges until what Jaspers calls the *Axial Period* (third stage) dated generally 800–200 B.C.

57

The most extraordinary events are concentrated in this period. Confucius and Lao-Tse were living in China. . . . India produced the Upanishads and Buddha and, like China, ran the whole gamut of philosophical possibilities down to scepticism, to materialism, sophism and nihilism; in Iran Zarathustra taught a challenging view of the world as a struggle between good and evil; in Palestine the prophets made their appearance, from Elijah, by way of Isaiah and Jeremiah to Deutero-Isaiah; Greece witnessed the appearance of Homer, of the philosophers—Parmenides, Heraclitus and Plato—of the tragedians, [of] Thucydides and Archimedes. Everything implied by those names developed during these few centuries simultaneously in China, India and the West, without any of those regions knowing of the others.[11]

According to Jaspers, mankind in each area has lived until now by recollection of the Axial Period. Certainly in India and China all the momentous questions were mooted then, and since then no new questions have been asked. As John Dewey takes his troubles to Plato, so in Jaspers' interpretation all mankind "returns in recollection to this period and is fired anew by it." Even in the West, until virtually the last two hundred years, thought was concerned with commutations and permutations of the same essential questions to which in effect all possible answers had been given before 200 B.C. It is only with the *scientific-technological age* (the fourth stage) that a new thing appears in the midst of the world and of men; and it appears, of necessity, in the West. (Jaspers affirms a necessary dependence, which we have already noticed, of the scientific attitude upon the Biblical doctrine of creation: the "Greek impulse to the closed form . . . paralyzes science;" whereas for Luther, for example, God "is present as Creator even in the intestines of a louse."[12]) It could appear only in the West because of certain unique elements in the Western complex of thought and life, which I shall refer to in a moment.

Obviously, a *schema* of this kind is subject to all kinds of criticism. But Jaspers is careful to insist that it is not presented as an all-embracing interpretation of history, for example of the Hegelian sort. This latter he considers an impossibility. He is not pretending to elucidate history's total *meaning*, but to identify certain epochs which are determinative of history's *structure* and, therefore, of the structure of our own minds.

It has this importance for our purpose: if we take some understanding of our own history to be vital to an understanding of ourselves, Jaspers helps us to pin point those parts of our history which are most momentous for this enterprise. Two things of a critical sort have, however, to be said. If it is true, as Jaspers acknowledges, that the "new" things which appear in the West have some kind of causal relation to the presence in the West not only of Hebrew (800–200 B.C.) but of Christian elements, then the end of the Western Axial period would have to be up-dated to A.D. 30 (or to A.D. 120 and the closing of the New Testament canon); for after all from the Christian point of view the event of Jesus Christ is the crown and climax of the prophetic history. Jaspers himself says: "For the consciousness of the West, Christ is the axis of history."[13] In the second place, there is no real explanation of these "new" things unless the Hebrew-Christian elements in the inheritance are distinguished more sharply than Jaspers distinguishes them from the Greek-Classical elements; for it can be argued with cogency, as for

59

example in Will Herberg's *Judaism and Modern Man*,[14] that Greek thought has more affinities with the Hindu-Buddhist complex than it has with the Biblical inheritance.

Nevertheless, even if the Jaspers account of the matter be subject to qualifications, to take it seriously, as I think we may, suggests that we shall find salient clues to the meaning of our own life and of our intellectual and moral constitution, if we pay attention to that complex of ideas which was generated during the Western Axial Period, and to the belated impact upon that development of the scientific outlook, which in its turn is closely interrelated with the growth of technology and industrialism.

For the balance of this chapter we shall speak of this Western heritage of ideas somewhat generally, and in the next chapter of the specific Biblical and Christian faith and its meaning.

In the nineteenth century attempts were made to write a detached or positivist history which would emancipate itself from Western prejudice and from the parochialism which assumes that world history has its center in the western European lands. Its postulate was that "battles between Negroes in the Sudan were on the same historical plane as Marathon or Salamis."[15] But this will not do. There have developed in the West, and only in the West, dynamisms powerful enough to impress themselves, for good or ill, even on India and China. And insofar as history is susceptible at all to the shaping force of ideas, the convictions which dominate even modern China were generated in the West. Dr. Mortimer Adler remarked recently on hearing a spokesman out of Asia lecture under the title, "The Yeast from the West"!

In his *Living Religions of the World*[16] Frederic Spiegelberg, who has no particular Christian ax to grind, insists that it is in the West and only in the West that mankind breaks from that view of history as endless recurrence which dominates Asian thought (and which also dominated Greek thought except where Biblical thought impinged upon it). It is, therefore, only in the West that there is the possibility of anything really *new*. The belief in a historical Incarnation[17] involves the belief that there is in history a real breakthrough into "newness of life", that mankind is no longer in bondage to what Paul calls "the elements of the world" (that is, to the dynamics of nature, which are involved in the *cycle*) but is free to go *somewhere* in obedience to the Divine impulse, and toward the Divinely appointed goal. By the same Divine act represented in the Incarnation man has restored to him his primordial dominion over the earth; he no longer fears the natural dynamisms, he scoffs at their demonic claims; and from this sovereignty over the natural order, from man's authorized determination to search it to its limits and subdue it to man's purposes, stems in the end of the day the fact of modern science.

> . . . the West, like the other great cultures, knows the dichotomy of human nature; on the one hand unrestrained life, on the other worldy mysticism—on the one hand the monsters, on the other the saints. But the West endeavors to rid itself of this dichotomy by finding the path that leads to the moulding of the world itself.[18]

While the *idea* of Incarnation is not absent from Asian thought, the idea of a *unique* Incarnation which gives to history a fulcrum and a center is impossible because of the cyclic view of life.

THE GREAT DEBATE

The unique character of Western thought and life develops from the fact that this Divine initiative thrusts against the ancient patterns—so that from the Axial Period onwards there is an endless yet fruitful debate, not only between the ancient beliefs as they appeared in Asia and in Greece, but between the whole Greco-Oriental complex (the term is Will Herberg's) and the affirmations stemming out of Hebrew-Christian faith. In this debate the significant human questions are canvassed and every possible answer proposed. We all bear on our intellectual bodies the scars of this debate; and so far is it from being true that the Christian thrust has conquered in the West, that in point of fact our mental and moral make-up is still largely shaped by classical thought, modified by the development of scientific logic, rather than by notions which are distinctively Christian.

Yet, setting aside for the moment the question of the truth or falsity of the Biblical and Christian reading of life, the debate itself is invigorating and enriching and can be illuminating insofar as we let its various currents play upon our own minds.

For example, we shall discover that we are all strongly marked with the influence of the dominant strain which we call very generally the *philosophia perennis* (the perennial philosophy), that persistent confidence in the competence of speculative reason and in the insight that thrusts beyond reason. It is because this strain is so dominant in our minds that we set such store by *knowledge*, both as *sophia* and as *gnosis*, both the wisdom of the mind and the wisdom that transcends mind. I have referred already to the uneasiness we feel when we notice that our moral convictions tend to be stronger than the *reasons* we can give for them. We have the instinct that this is a somewhat disreputable situation, that our convictions ought not to be stronger than our reasons, and that if they are we must either buttress our reasons or qualify our convictions. Our loyalties, so we have been taught to think, have only as much validity as can be given them by philosophic or scientific logic. They must be either rationally self-evident or rationally demonstrable—or they are suspect. This whole strain of conviction means that we are heirs of an inheritance, and that one particular part of our inheritance tends to determine our way of looking at the world. The Hebrews, for example, if such a dilemma had ever occurred to them, would have stuck with the convictions and postponed or done without the reasons. It is as children of Athens that we are all rationalists; and as heirs of the scientific tradition we are still rationalists, but more empirically-minded even than Aristotle. The knowledge on which life is to be grounded must be either speculative, having to do with timeless or rationally self-validating truth—or it must be scientific.

John Dewey set out in order the options which for most of us are taken for granted:

> . . . the measure of the worth of knowledge according to Aristotle . . . is the degree to which it is purely contemplative. . . .
>
> Through this taking over of the conception of knowledge as contemplative . . . multitudes are affected who are totally innocent of theoretical philosophy. . . . So deeply ingrained was this idea that it prevailed for centuries after the actual progress of science had demonstrated that knowledge is power to transform the world,

and centuries after the practice of effective knowledge had adopted the method of experimentation.[19]

These are the two methods which we take for granted must be applicable to every question under heaven, or in heaven: the existence of God and the demands of duty must prove themselves either by rational consistency or by experimental demonstration. The trouble is that the demands of life are always running ahead of the possibility of demonstration: "We have to believe prematurely in order that we may act expeditiously," as Ralph Barton Perry somewhere says. And more than that: it appears that the very basic affirmations on which we actually ground our living—like the worth of life or the value of freedom—are none of them susceptible either to rational or experimental verification. And just as in the ancient world, when the adequacy of reason to give knowledge of reality was called in question men turned from the schools of philosophy to the shrines of the Mysteries, so in our own day we have a movement to religions of initiation and to techniques of intuition. An example at random is Aldous Huxley's commendation of mescal, which drug apparently has the trick of suspending the normal restraints of logic, of cutting beneath and beyond the normal processes of subject-object thinking and opening the way to direct and intuitive perception, in which reality may be touched and smelled with an immediacy which intoxicates not the senses but the man.[20]

Contemplative reason dissolves reality away; scientific reason splits it to the destruction of meaning. We can reach it in its integrity—so the ancient and the modern Gnostics unite to tell us—only by the suspension of our humanity *and* of our reason.

This strain of rationalism pushing into Gnosticism is one

element in our inheritance, and we are inexplicable to ourselves without it. From this source also derives our inclination to assume that the test of every proposed solution of the problem of life is its capacity to provide *illumination*, to supply us either with timeless truths and principles in the light of which life may be rightly ordered, or with practical knowledge of the structures of the world, by means of which knowledge life may be prudently conducted. There is a strong tendency to assume that the significance of Jesus, for example, must rest on his unique capacity to supply insight into the meaning of the true and the good. The central Christian affirmation that He comes less to communicate insight *to* man than to do something *for* men is assumed to be an irrelevance, and probably a Pauline invention. The assumption is that if men know the truth they will acknowledge it; if they know the good they will do it. We are still dominated by the Platonic notion that men are rationally competent to apprehend the truth, and morally competent to obey it. In the perspective of Biblical faith, on the other hand, men characteristically deny the truth they know; and the problem of the moral life is not that men do not know the good but that, knowing it, they do not perform it. Their problem *begins* when they know the good.

Together with the tradition which gives one confidence in reason and in knowledge, we are heirs also of a more skeptical tradition, which questions the pretensions of reason and is suspicious of every vaunted *gnosis*, a tradition which emphasizes the qualified and conditioned character of all our insights. This tradition of cynicism has always been alive and active, but it has been recovered and reinforced by the development of the human and social sciences, which analyze the biological and social matrix out of which speculation

65

arises and emphasize the degree to which our thought is bound and not free. It is impossible since Marx to ignore the fact that if we are to tell the truth about man we must pay attention to what goes on in his stomach as well as in his head, and that what goes on in his head is intimately related to what goes on in his stomach: that a man will not think straight on an empty stomach, nor much better on a full one. This insight of course is not unique to Marx; it was Samuel Butler who said, "The healthy stomach is nothing if not conservative. Few radicals have good digestions." Further, it is impossible since Freud to deny that there is a clear and in a measure describable connection between the brain cells and the sex glands; that at the very least the clear current of thought is sullied by deposits of prejudice churned up by a predatory sex.

If one thing is clear in the light of the naturalistic and scientific tradition, it is that the ancient imperative "Know thyself" is a good deal more exacting than a discipline in introspection. All our judgments, including our judgments about ourselves, including also our rational and moral affirmations, are biologically, psychologically, and sociologically conditioned, desperately limited, and potentially misleading.

The imperative "Know thyself" is never completely obeyed, but our hesitant compliances do lead to ever new understandings of the limits as well as of the possibilities of the mind. History and sociology have continued the human self-criticism which psychology began. They have taught us that we are not only beings whose intelligence is conditioned by sensation, interest and feeling, but that we are also beings whose concepts are something less than the concepts of a universal reason.[21]

This is putting it very mildly. The human fact is that conviction is emasculated and the moral impulse debilitated by this recognition of the relativity of all judgment. The same tradition which generates our hankering after rational confidence teaches us also the shaky character of all such confidence. We are historically conditioned to yearn for the absolute, yet caught by the nature of our more recent heritage in the swamp of rational and moral relativism. The problem is not so much that we don't know enough about our interior moral and intellectual chemistry; the problem is that we live at the junction of conflicting cultural and intellectual movements. Our dilemma arises less out of our psyche than out of our history.

In the following chapter I shall argue that in the providence of God we are not left halting between these two options: an absolutism which would claim to know more than can be known by men limited as all men are; and a relativism which would end by proposing that we can know nothing at all (not even, possibly, that relativism is true). Meanwhile, there is space only for the reminder that there is a third strain in the complex heritage—the Biblical faith which is part of that heritage yet in a strange way not part of it. It presents itself not as one of the options which occur to men when they reflect deeply upon the nature of the world and the depths of their own life, but as a hard fact in the midst of the world which forces us to broaden the alternatives, and to accept it that the rational options are not the only options. Yet while it insists that the rational options are not the only options, it refuses that flight from the world of rational and moral activity which is the way of transrational *gnosis*. It recognizes, for example, the limitations on reason which are insisted on by the human and social sciences and proposes even further limits of its own; but it does not then propose that reason should be either transcended by mysticism or abandoned in nihilism, but *restored* by being ensconced in love and humility and chastened by a recognition of its own limits. It knows that man's reason is always less reasonable than men claim it to be, yet proposes a "right reason" which is rid of the poison of pride in reason and of the pride that perverts reason. It can believe that man is a rational animal, while reminding him that he is never as rational as he pretends. It knows and cherishes man's rational endowment yet will not put too much store by it, since it knows that man's life including man's reason is in bondage to "the beggarly elements of the world" (partially represented in Marx's "ensemble of the social relations"); that his judgment is bent continually by interest, greed, and fear. Yet it will not on this account abandon hope for man or for the world, since it knows of resources powerful enough to redeem both. It can take account of conflicting views of history—that history is the history of thought (Collingwood); that history is the history of class struggle (Marx)—and comprehend both in a conception of history, and of the sovereignty of God in history, which takes seriously both the play of ideas and the conflict of economic classes, both man's head and man's stomach. Yet it will place the meaning of history and the hope of salvation in neither the one nor the other.

About the tradition in general there is this to be said. Immersion in the cultural inheritance, even if we extend the range of our study to take in myriad strains which are not even mentioned here, will not tell us infallibly the truth about man. It is possible to master it—and still to believe either that man is a kind of cosmic eczema ("a pestiferous rash upon the face of nature") or a son of the most high God. Both can be believed; both have been believed. It will not even tell us infallibly the truth about ourselves, unless we can lay hold of some one element in it that makes sense of all the rest. But it does help us to understand the mixed elements in us that make us men, and which make us the kind of men we are. It will not give us one single inescapable version of what it means to live a human life, but it will help us to understand what the alternatives are and save us from false simplifications. It will save us, too, from the wasteful vanity of inventing new heresies, as we discover that our most outlandish inventions are very ancient indeed. We will not be tempted to think, for example, when the problem of the relativity of all morals hits us between the eyes, that this awesome discovery was new to the Church until we got it from our sociology professor. We shall not take our discovery of the vexing question of free will and determinism to mean that we stand in the vanguard of speculation, nor will we confuse determinism with the theological idea of predetermination—not if we have had a look at Augustine and Pelagius, or at Luther and Erasmus. After we have read them, we may even be content to let them state the issues for us.

The more comprehensive our knowledge of the inheritance, the less likely we shall be to fall into any one of three quite disastrous errors:

1) The first is, clearly, to imagine that we have to begin the quest for self-understanding from scratch, as it were. If the members of the morose and abortive bull session to which I referred at the beginning of the book would begin from the sources instead of from their own confused insights and insides they would have at least the zest of real exploration under experienced guides, and even, *Deo volente,* the

exultation of real discovery. Our labored exploration of the meaning of our humanity can be aided inestimably if we use the maps left us by Plato and Augustine, by Erasmus and by Marx. And we have, as a bonus, the satisfaction of correcting one by the other.

2) The second is to take one element in the inheritance overseriously, and to pin too much on it. The idealists and the nominalists, the mystics and materialists cannot all be right; in fact most of them must most of the time be wrong. Therefore we shall walk gratefully but somewhat gingerly in the house of the mind that they have furnished for us. And when we notice how susceptible to error are even the best and wisest of men, we shall acquire a wholesome sense of the provisional quality of our own most cherished notions. Possibly as important: we shall acquire that salutary skepticism about the admonitions of the elders which Max Otto, as we saw, thinks we already have. We shall, in fine, beware of easy dogmatisms whether they come sanctified by age or blinding us with their pristine newness. Especially we shall be wary of simple formulas about the nature of man which, if they are simple enough to be enticing, probably have no more validity than that they jibe with our own prejudice.

3) The third is to romanticize the inheritance as a whole, which is possible only at the price of confusion of mind. We shall examine in Chapter IV a somewhat striking and influential instance of that.

The function of tradition is to stretch the mind and not to shape it, to force our thought, and especially our thought about ourselves, out of the rut of our mental habit and out beyond the limits of our own capacity for self-dissection and self-analysis. Especially it helps us to transcend the fashion of our generation, since, in spite of the limits upon ancestral wisdom, the generations are likely to be wiser than any one of them: "the world is wiser than the moderns," as G. K. Chesterton puts it with his usual epigrammatic precision.

In any event the options are clear: we can have a life void of self-understanding because it is devoid of that knowledge of our history without which our selves are obscure to ourselves; or we can have, at least in some measure, that knowledge of the self which is conditional upon a knowledge of our history. Mark well that a summons to take our inheritance seriously does not at all mean conformism or conservatism; it is in fact the condition of freedom. For if it be true that "freedom is the knowledge of necessity," as in some sense it is, then the knowledge of the historic forces which shape our judgments and make our minds is the precondition of responsible decision.

Serious and devoted attention to our inheritance is a kind of enlarged patriotism; and, like patriotism, it is not enough. It can tell us what makes us tick, but it cannot tell us what time to keep. It can tell us *what* we are and help us understand why we are confused about *who* we are, but it will not itself get rid of the confusion. It is at this point that Christianity has something of its own to say.

NOTES TO CHAPTER II

1. Niebuhr, H. Richard: *The Meaning of Revelation*. The Macmillan Company, New York, 1946, p. 48.
2. Otto, Max: *Science and the Moral Life*. Mentor Books, 1949, pp. 40–42.
3. Books of importance on the matter are, among others, Niebuhr, Reinhold: *Faith and History*, Shinn: *Christianity and the Problem of History*, Butterfield: *Christianity and History*.

4. *Orthodoxy*. Dodd, Mead & Company, Inc., New York, 1952, p. 85.
5. Niebuhr, Reinhold: *The Self and the Dramas of History*. Charles Scribner's Sons, New York, 1955, p. 15. (This corresponds with Camus' analysis of the psychology of *The Rebel* in the book of that name.)
6. Various accounts in various *Lives*. This from Santillana: *The Age of Adventure*. p. 91.
7. Collingwood, R. G: *The Idea of History*. Clarendon Press, Oxford, 1946, pp. 35–36.
8. Rupp, Gordon: *Principalities and Powers*. Abingdon-Cokesbury Press, Nashville, 1952. (This book might well have been added under Note 3 above. It is a brief but very graphic and readable account of the Christian view of history.)
9. Voegelin, Eric: *The New Science of Politics*. University of Chicago Press, 1952, p. 78.
10. Jaspers, Karl: *The Origin and Goal of History*. Yale University Press, New Haven, 1953, p. 28.
11. *Ibid.*, p. 2.
12. *Ibid.*, p. 91.
13. *Ibid.*, p. 58.
14. Herberg, Will: *Judaism and Modern Man*. Farrar, Straus & Young, Inc., New York, 1951.
15. Jaspers: *op. cit.*, p. xiv.
16. Spiegelberg, Frederic: *Living Religions of The World*. Prentice-Hall, Inc., New York, 1956.
17. Spiegelberg says that the notion of a "datable" Incarnation was congenial to the West because for the West history "already" was thought of in a linear rather than a circular way. By "already" he can only refer to Biblical and prophetic thought.
18. Jaspers: *op. cit.*, pp. 63–64.
19. Dewey, John: *Reconstruction in Philosophy*. Mentor Books, 1950, pp. 99–100.
20. Huxley, Aldous: *The Doors of Perception*. Harper & Brothers, New York, 1954.
21. Niebuhr, H. Richard: *op. cit.*, p. 9.

CHAPTER III

The Mirror of Christ

> Among the infinite variety of life's phenom-
> ena some moment or object or person stands
> out as uniquely significant and revealing,
> providing a clue to the character of the whole.
> Some item of experience, or group of items,
> impresses the mind so deeply as to operate
> as a spiritual catalyst. . . . In Christianity
> the catalyst of faith is the person of Jesus
> Christ.[1]
>
> JOHN HICK

Christ as *mirror, catalyst, axis* (to go back to Jaspers' word):
the figures are various, but the intention is to say that in some
sense the person of Jesus Christ is crucial for our understanding both of history and of life—and of our own life. That is
the assertion I want to make and validate; but since it may be,
in the first instance, highly implausible, let me begin by
listing some preliminary reasons for taking it seriously:

1) Whether or not it be true that Christ is crucial and
Christianity is true, I think we have to accept the fact that
without Christ and Christianity the Western world would

73

not be the same and that, therefore, we would not be the kind of men we are. We are, for good or ill, *Homo Christianus* as well as *Homo Classicus* and all the rest. We share a Christian heritage even if we think it an incubus; and it is vital to understand it even if we have in mind to abandon it.

2) The contemporary intellectual discussion increasingly centers on the Christian claim, so that it is possible for a first-class epistemologist like John Hick to declare that Christ is the clue to all knowledge, and for a front-rank philosopher of history like Karl Jaspers to insist that "For the consciousness of the West, Christ is the axis of history"; not only so, but it has become commonplace that literary analysts of culture like Faulkner *(The Fable)* and Camus *(The Fall)* find their themes among the Christian themes. They may or may not handle them in a Christian way, but the effect of it all is that Christianity with surprising resilience takes the center of the intellectual arena once again. That does not make it true; it does make it worth attention.

3) The Lecturer stands within the circle of faith drawn by the founders of the Lectureship, sharing their conviction that the Christian faith is true, and that our lives miss their meaning if its truth is neglected or denied.

Whether or not, then, history moves on the axis of Christ, the intention is that this book should do so! The first chapter was concerned with showing that the understanding of the self is a matter of history rather than of introspection; the second that history sketches alternatives but dictates no conclusion. The present chapter is dedicated to the proposition that the real man and the true self is not the natural man or the rational man or the economic man—though man is all of these. The true man, the *"proper* Man" in Luther's great phrase, is One Man, Jesus Christ. (The word *proper* is sadly disfigured in our usage. By derivation it does not mean, as we use it, conventional or acceptable but *normative*. The root *proprio* gives us our *appropriate*, in the sense of fitting; so that the *proper man* is true man, free of distortion or perversion. *Integral* is near it, with its derivative *integrity*, meaning *whole*.) We are our true selves in the measure in which we are rightly related to Him (*con-formed* to Him as the New Testament puts it); therefore the proper measure of mankind is not *man* but the *new man* in Christ. The Christian element in our inheritance, therefore, is not merely one element but the critical element; the Christian history is the clue to all history and, therefore, to our understanding of ourselves.

There you have, if you like, the conclusion before the argument, the proposition which I am now committed to defend. The argument follows; and the remaining chapters of the book deal with contemporary, intellectual, moral, and social issues in the light of that understanding of human nature, and of our nature, which derives from the Christian proclamation concerning Jesus Christ.

We are not only Homo Classicus, l'homme bourgeois, and so on; we are all, quite specifically, Homo Christianus, at least in the sense that we belong in a Christian society. I do not mean that our society, or we ourselves individually, give explicit adherence to the Christian Gospel; but, whether we do or do not, it is most certainly true that it is from the Christian inheritance that there comes in large part that mesh of loves and loyalties, and of guilt for broken loyalties, which both sustains and torments us all. From this entailment not one of us is exempt; we are all Hebrews, we are all Catholics, we are all Puritans, in the real measure in which

Moses and Augustine and Richard Baxter have had a hand in shaping the moral mind of the West and of this land, and so of our moral minds. It is true of all of us: even of that scruffy crowd of hooligans who, several weeks ago in California, staged a kangaroo court in a jail drunk tank and hanged a fellow inmate because, so they said, he was "unsociable." Even the perverse value they set on sociability, and the court procedures they so cruelly mimicked, they owed unwittingly to a Christian culture which, if they knew of it, they would indubitably spit upon.

It is true of all of us, even of those who live out on the rebel fringe of our society; but it may also be true that the Christian elements are stronger in inverse proportion to our sophistication. At least this probably was true during the long period when *classic* meant Greece and Rome, and when a classical, which is to say a liberal, education meant a learned emancipation from the Bible. We are victims of what Father John Courtney Murray called

> . . . those absurd prejudices . . . which banish from the blessed world of educational curricula a number of authors on the pretext that they are not "classical." The writings of the Fathers of the Church are an integral part of the humanities as well as, or more than, those of the Elizabethan dramatists.

As William Pollard of the Oak Institute of Nuclear Studies said at the same conference:

> . . . the student may study history from the ancient world to the present . . . but . . . the great Biblical themes of redemption and judgment in history, of freedom and grace and sin . . . seem strangely vague, far away, and

76

unrelated to the ebb and flow of life and history as he understands it.[2]

Whether the Christian themes have until now seemed intimately present and illuminating, or remote and irrelevant, we have now another opportunity to decide whether the Christian inheritance is an incubus from which we would want to be free, or a profound resource which we would want to explore, specifically in the interest of the understanding of the self and of ourselves. Before we decide to dismiss it or embrace it, let us make a new attempt at understanding what it is.

CHRISTIANITY AS HISTORY AND COMMUNITY

I was having a snack a while ago at the counter in a café near Stanford University—a cup of coffee in one hand and, as it happened, a volume of Church History in the other. A character on my right leaned over me and said in a lugubrious voice: "Church history is fine, but *do you have the love of God in your heart?*" He was perfectly serious and his question perfectly legitimate, though I suppose that there is a time and place for everything. Probably a sound reply would have been: "That's a good question, but the love of God works not only in our hearts but in the world; and Church History is the story of the love of God in action." Not that every book on Church History reads that way. There are some: Charles Williams' *The Descent of the Dove*, which I have referred to already, is at once a first-rate Church History and a hymn to the love of God. We shall see later (as Williams sees) that there is much more and much worse in

Church History than the love of God; but sadly as Church History is disfigured by the sin of man and the activity of Satan, it is still in its essence the chronicle of Divine activity. Yet to be seen that way it must be seen, as any living tradition must be seen if it is to yield its real meaning, from inside. It *can* be looked at from within or from without. Take, for example, the case quoted by Richard Niebuhr in his *The Meaning of Revelation:*[3] it concerns the signing of the Declaration of Independence. From outside, in the *Cambridge Modern History* version, it looked like this:

> On July 4, 1776, Congress passed the resolution which made the colonies independent communities, issuing at the same time the well-known Declaration of Independence. If we regard the Declaration as the assertion of an abstract political theory, criticism and condemnation are easy. It sets out with a general proposition so vague as to be practically useless. The doctrine of the equality of man, unless it be qualified and conditioned by reference to special circumstance, is either a barren truism or a delusion.

while from inside, as Lincoln saw it from the field at Gettysburg, it looked like this:

> Fourscore and seven years ago our fathers brought forth upon this continent a new nation, conceived in liberty and dedicated to the proposition that all men are created equal.

This is not merely, as Niebuhr says, "the blind devotion of a patriot" opposed to the critical acumen and dispassionate judgment of the scientific historian.

The disparity goes deeper . . . the "Congress" is one thing, "our fathers" are almost another reality. The proposition

that all men are created free and equal, to which the
fathers dedicated their lives, their fortunes and their sacred
honor, seems to belong to a different order of ideas than
that to which the vague and useless, barren truism or
delusion belong.

But to see it Lincoln's way you have to be an American, or
at least by an effort of imagination you have to make the
American vision your own. To an American the proposition
is indisputable; it could be denied only by ceasing to be an
American. And it puts its power on such a man not by its
logical cogency but because it is a part of his history, and
because it helps him understand what it means that he *is*
an American. And because I am not an American, let me
make the same point on a less solemn level by telling a story
which the President of my own University brought back out
of Britain. He met, said he, on the Atlantic crossing, a gentleman who told him of an American who had made repeated
trips to Britain and cherished a profound love for the place.
But he had never achieved what was his prime ambition: to
own and wear an English suit of clothes. So on his latest trip
he hied himself to Savile Row and was duly measured. He
went back for repeated fittings, as is the English way, and
finally had the glad word that the suit was finished and
awaited his approval. He put it on, revolved before the
mirror, and pronounced himself delighted. The cloth was as
he had dreamt it, the fit left nothing to be desired. Then the
tailor brought out two packages. "We always provide two
gifts," said he, "for our overseas customers." And he produced
a Derby hat and a rolled-up umbrella. The customer donned
the hat, hung the umbrella on his arm, turned again to the
mirror, and to the tailor's dismay burst into tears. "My dear

79

sir, whatever is the matter?" said the tailor, "Are you disappointed in the suit after all?" "No, no," said the American customer, "but . . . but isn't it dreadful that we've lost Indiah!" The implied political comment is not accurate, but the point is sound: that to know the ~~feel~~ of a tradition from inside we actually have to ~~be inside~~ it, to step, as it were, into its clothes. Martin Buber's way of putting it is that to know what it means to be a Jew, for example, it is not enough to study a set of ideas: you must, as he puts it, "take part in the tribal dance;" you must get inside the meaning of the ritual and the discipline and the celebration.

Now by the grace of heaven we all have in some measure this relation to Christianity. We all take part in the tribal dance, if only out of courtesy. We celebrate Christmas, we go through many of the motions of Christian morality. The trouble is that the pattern has grown formal, habitual. Shall we drop the mummery or try to bring the thing alive?

This approach to the matter is so unfamiliar, as far as my experience goes, that we must try to make it somewhat clearer. The common assumption is that religion, and Christianity in particular, is essentially a set of ideas, and that when a religion claims to be true it claims that it is the custodian of a truer set of ideas than its rivals can boast of. Now this is simply not so of Christianity. It is not even true of the word religion in its derivation. For *religio* (the root means *to bind*: *li*gature, *li*gament, ob*li*gation), in its Roman origin, referred not to a philosophy of life but to the tradition of the Roman people. Roman religion was family lore rather than philosophy: it was the bond (the ligature) that tied a man to his community.

The Roman sense of historical tradition was not a philosophical deduction; it was a psychological necessity to a race of peasants. The family is knit together by blood and a common land turned over by hands that had received their patrimony from a line of ancestors stretching back to the youth of the race. The dusk falls on the back of each man as he retreats down the road of time; but as he has received from the past, so has he given to the future; and as they lived in him, so shall he live in them. And this is promised him by the household gods, and even when he no longer believes in his gods, he keeps them, because they are the badge of his service, and the pledge of his immortality.[4]

This is pagan; but when we use the word *religion* we should know that this, in its origin, is what it means. To move into the world of ideas is to move *out of* the world of religion. Living religion, in the normal experience of mankind, is history and tradition. From there are generated the values that man lives by; there in his history are the objects of his loyalty, the cherished "gods" by which he guides his life.

In order to *be* at all, an absolute must become a family heirloom.[5]

"As a rule men are polytheists . . . Sometimes they live for Jesus' God, sometimes for country and sometimes for Yale"[6] (or Harvard, or Stanford); but some god they do have, and they derive that loyalty not from the thin air of speculation, but from the rich matrix of history and experience.

To be a self is to have a god; to have a god is to have history . . . to have one god is to have one history. God and history of selves in community belong together in inseparable union.[7]

81

This is true, a fortiori, of Christianity. To be a Christian is not to have special contemplative or rational insight into the nature of Being; it is to be incorporated into a specific community, with specific origins and a living history. In his novel *The Cardinal* Henry Morton Robinson tells of Din the Boston carman who as he passed the church each day, and sixteen times a day, tipped his cap and gravely bowed to the Presence tabernacled there. Not for his very life could Din have told you the metaphysical "how" of the Presence; what he was celebrating was not his assent to a proposition but his membership in a historic community of faith which, as he understood it, had Christ at its heart. Christian theology, when it is true to itself, is not primarily a contribution to intellectual discussion but an explanation in and to a community of the origin and meaning of its own historic life. It gives off metaphysical sparks, it has rational implications as wide as all philosophy, but its prime reference is not to philosophy but to history.

This is, indeed, a world removed from the near-mysticism of the perennial philosophy, from the truth both of speculation and contemplation. But man is not made for the bloodless abstractions of metaphysics, but for the vivid life of history and community. The condition of knowledge of the one thing needful—and surely it is a reassuring condition—is not ontological sophistication but faithfulness to the demands of human and social life. God is not the god of the philosophers, as Pascal knew, but the God of Abraham, Isaac, and Jacob—the living God, who does not wait to be discovered at the end of the philosopher's quest, but who gives himself to be known in the midst of human affairs. The condition of knowledge is not the enlightened mind but the open and passionate heart. There is a place for speculation and an honorable role for the enlightened mind; but man was not born to paddle in the shallows of timeless truths and ontological speculation, but to swim in the deep waters of compassion.

THE FACT OF CHRIST

We have argued thus far that without the knowledge of our history we are inexplicable to ourselves, but that while history is rich in illumination of the ingredients that make us what we are, it is itself such a complex and mixed-up business that it is small wonder that we ourselves are a riddle to ourselves. A crazy mixed-up history produces, not surprisingly and not to put too fine a point on it, crazy mixed-up kids. And so we need something in history to tie to, something which will give meaning to the whole and to ourselves. The fact that the situation cries for such a "something" does not mean that the needed clue is there; but it may win some attention for the Christian claim that there is in history precisely such a thin red line of meaning. "The truth about history is not equally revealed in all history,"[8] but is revealed, according to the Christian claim, in the community life of the people of God, which is the theme of the Old Testament Scriptures, which comes to sharp and tragic-triumphant focus in the New Testament (the true Axial Period in a Christian reading of the matter) and is continued in the history of the Christian Church.

So far so good; but we are left with the dilemma that the history of the Christian Church is itself compact of confusion. It is itself crazy, mixed up, compound of shame and of glory, of extraordinary triumph and of dismal failure, of matchless compassion and of shameful pride. It is not only

83

that the good is conjoined with evil, but that the good becomes itself an occasion for evil. The gift of revelation becomes an excuse for pride in knowledge; the unmerited grace which brought the Church into being becomes a claim to special merit; the humility to which men are summoned in the Gospel becomes, perversely, "I thank thee, Lord, that I am not as other men are . . . proud." There are cheap jibes in plenty about the hypocrites in the Church, but the fact ought to be faced that the Church is a very nursery of hypocrisy, if only because the role which it delineates for itself is so demanding that the thing turns into a masquerade. The profession is so high that sometimes the profession is mistaken for the performance, the word for the action. Evil nourishes itself in the soil of the good, so that in the community born of the knowledge of God the knowledge which should destroy pride becomes an occasion for pride and a cloak for egoism. In *The Devils of Loudun* Aldous Huxley can say of the Abbé Grandier:

> A long religious training had not abolished or even mitigated his self-love; it had served only to provide the ego with a theological alibi. The untutored egoist merely wants what he wants. Give him a theological education, and it becomes obvious to him, it becomes axiomatic, that what *he* wants is what God wants.[9]

This is not news to those of us who are familiar with the occupational hazards of the seminary and the ministry, but it is wholesome if not palatable to be reminded of it.

Speaking of the Inquisition, Charles Williams says:

> The Church committed herself, on the highest possible principles, to the breach of the highest possible princi-

ples. . . . Deep, deeper than we believe, lie the roots of evil; it is in the good that they exist; it is in the good that they thrive and send up sap and produce the black fruit of hell.[10]

And because the point is worth emphasizing and the quotation is worth quoting, here is Montaigne:

Our zeal performs wonders when it seconds our inclinations to hatred, cruelty, ambition, avarice, detraction, rebellion. . . .[11]

To all these moral ills the Christian flesh is heir; and the social body of the Church is no less susceptible to corruption —by the spirit of the age, by the fear of vested interests and the fear *for* its own interest. For the elixir of life is substituted the opium of the people; and the prophetic and apostolic Word is muted, too often, by querulousness and worse.

No, Christian history is not, in the large sense and as a whole, Divine revelation: the saving Word and the Divine activity is too closely joined to and intermixed with the sin which it challenges. If there is Divine truth and Divine activity here, it makes itself known and accomplishes its work as much in spite of the Church as because of it. So that always when the Church knows what it is about it points away from itself; or rather it points to that Mystery at its heart, that luminous point so desperately obscured by the Church's own wretchedness, that Fact without which the Church itself in its glory *and* its wretchedness is inexplicable to itself—the Fact of Jesus Christ.

THE AXIS OF HISTORY

So the focus narrows still further: from history in general to a particular history, and from a particular history which is itself filled with confusion and contradiction to a single Fact which explains not only the history but also the confusion—the Man Christ Jesus who is the embodiment (Incarnation) of the judgment and of the mercy of God. The approach of Christianity to the problem of history is not that of classical philosophy, which sought universals at the price of abstraction; or of science, which seeks generalizations by the endless accumulation of instances. For the necessary understanding of our own history and therefore of ourselves, Christianity proposes (to use a figure of Gordon Rupp's) the microscope rather than the telescope.

[The Christian] turns from the methods of the telescope to those of the microscope; he turns to the field of biblical history. He points to the circumscribed area of Jewish national history, to the little land of Palestine, and to the story of a Semitic tribe which over much of its life and for most of the time does not seem to differ greatly from its neighbours. When we turn from the Old Testament to the New, the concentration is still more remarkable. We are asked to pick out one grain of sand from the great sandheap of humanity, to look at the life of one single man. . . . The Gospel narratives . . . slip rapidly over thirty years. They fasten on rather less than three years, and within this period on a few months, and within this on one week, and finally on events in two days which are evidently conceived to be of such importance that they are described to us, hour by hour.[12]

86

We shall not tackle all the problems raised by this approach to the meaning of history and of life, but there are several things to be said about this *prismatic* view of history:

1) It implies that the truth about history is personal and dramatic rather than metaphysical or statistical (empirical). And that just as in any significant drama the meaning of the story may be focused, and generally is, in one climactic, clarifying moment, so with the human and historic tale. It simply transfers to history what is true of our personal lives: that we derive our best insight into their meaning, not from reflection upon the whole, but from those crucial and life-shaping encounters which open up the meaning of life in its depth. "Falling in love" is of course the prototype experience: the clarifying, emancipating surrender of the self to the glad bondage of another, the revelation of the spuriousness of the self-centered life, the transmutation of values which is involved in the unreserved commitment of the self to the beloved. The Christian contention is plainly that the Passion of Christ is in some such way the clarifying center of Everyman's life. It is history in depth: not ontological depth, mark you, but the depth of love, wherein is opened up the exceeding sinfulness of sin, and where is made known the love of Christ which passeth ontological knowledge.

2) The kind of knowledge of history and destiny which is opened up *here* is accessible to all men equally. It requires no speculative aptitude, no scientific training, no vast accumulation of historic learning. The condition of apprehension is not sophistication but what the Bible calls *simplicity*, and for which our word would probably be *integrity* (or in the jargon, *existential commitment*). The vital logic of the matter is that the more deeply we are involved in the living of life, the more profoundly the meaning of the life we live will be

illuminated by the Divine prismatic focusing of righteousness and love. Here is the true "still center of the turning
world": not the stillness of reflection, but the throbbing beat
of Divine compassion unmastered by human sin. "The light
shineth in darkness, and the darkness does not overwhelm it."

3) To be a Christian, then, is not to have a more con-
vincing philosophy of life, more proofs for the existence of
God, better answers to vexing questions than other men have.
Books which compare Jesus with "other founders of the
great world religions" are misconceived. Jesus is not the
founder of a "religion" in the accepted sense of that term; he
could only be so regarded from the "outside." He comes
actually late in a living tradition, in the "fullness of the time."
His "insights" are not original and he expressly disclaims that
they are. He comes not to establish a new philosophy of life
but to fulfill the promises of God, to gather into burning
focus the fragmentary manifestations of God's love in the
midst of the world. He is the first-born of a New Humanity,
the fruit of that Love which in his own broken body pours
itself out utterly.

That is why the intellectual argument for the existence of
God is always peripheral, where it figures at all, in Christian
proclamation. Even the late and greatly lamented Father
Ronald Knox, a convert to a tradition in which the "proofs"
figure somewhat prominently, says of them that they do little
more than help carry over those periods of spiritual barren-
ness when the vision of the glory of God in the face of Christ
grows dull and dim. In such times it is some reassurance to
remember that it is logically very difficult to get rid of God:
but the logic at best buttresses faith; it does not normally
create it. The more normal reaction of Christian faith would
be that to talk about proofs for the existence of God at this

late date in the history of the Christian Church is rather like inviting a man who has been married for thirty years to prove that his wife exists. When the good Lord has been busy lo these many years, judging his people, making good on his promises, sending his prophets and in the fullness of time his Son, it is a bit late in the day to raise the question of his existence. The Christian's faith is grounded—like a man's faith in his wife—not in the cogency of logic but in the consistency of love. It is generated, like every personal loyalty, from a level deeper than logic. It is no more susceptible of rational demonstration or of rational rebuttal than a man's faith in his wife. He does not wait to pledge himself to her until he has solved the ontological problem of her existence, though since he loves her he will be interested in everything about her; but the love is primary, the questions are secondary. And so it is with the relation of the community of faith to the living God whose love brought it into being.

I am staggered often by the superficial way in which the question about God is put; students tell me in bull session, as I understand them, that if I will clear up the questions— about free will and predestination, about the fate of unbaptized children in the hinterland of Africa—they are prepared to consider the possibility of believing in God. There are answers to the questions,[18] but they can wait on an answer to the prior question: Since "to be a self is to have a God," is the god to whose service our life is devoted the true God or an idol? In fact the questions *must* wait upon that question, since that is a question to which we give our answer simply by drawing breath and by living life.

To make Christian history our history, it should be noticed, is not to abstract ourselves from general history. To find in Christ the human and sacred image is not to cut ourselves off from the generality of mankind. Actually this essential orthodoxy is the liberating precondition of our being at home in the world, and of our being kin to all men. There is in Greenwich, England, a final yardstick of all yard measures, and in Paris a "Paris meter"; by these *orthodox* (which is not mistranslated to mean *right measure*) measures all other pretended yardsticks are to be tested: and there is a sense in which to accept this is to know where we are—*anywhere.*

What needs to be said here has, I think, best been said by H. Richard Niebuhr in *The Meaning of Revelation.*[14]

To Christians the revelatory moment is not only something they can all remember as having happened in their own past, be they Hebrews or Greeks, slaves or free, Europeans or Africans or Americans or Asiatics, mediaeval men or modern. It becomes an occasion for appropriating as their own the past of all human groups. Through Jesus Christ Christians of all races recognize the Hebrews as their fathers; they build into their lives as Englishmen or Americans, as Italians or Germans, the memories of Abraham's loyalty, of Moses' heroic leadership, of prophetic denunciations and comfortings. All that has happened to the strange and wandering people of God becomes a part of their own past. But Jesus Christ is not only the Jew who suffered for the sins of Jews and for our own sins; he is also the member of the Roman world-community through whom the Roman past is made our own. . . . Beyond all that, he is the man through whom the whole of human history becomes our history. Now there is nothing that is alien to us. All the struggles, searchings after light, all the wanderings of the peoples, all the sins of men in all places become parts of our past through him.

But it is not only that the event of Christ illuminates in its depth the meaning of the past; it pulls into intelligible focus "all the occasions of personal and common life." It does not enable us to foretell the future, as would a philosophy of history or a scientific history were such available; but by lighting up the truth of life it does prevent our being taken by surprise.

Before we move on from here, I ought to say a word about the so-called "scandal of particularity" involved in all this. I don't know how to make it "plausible" that God should reveal himself in Christ in a literally *singular*[15] way; but the alternative, which so many people find appealing, seems to me singularly unpersuasive. It involves a turning away from the uniqueness of the Scriptural story, from the burning bush of Moses, and the Cross aflame with love, to affirm that "every common bush" is aflame with God. But into the minds of people who claim to see God everywhere I simply cannot enter. Daniel Jenkins suggests[16] that they must surely be very sheltered people. Buddha and Marx differed widely, but on one thing they were agreed: that they had looked deep into life and history and did not see God there at all. The papers only today (September 13, 1957) carry the story of a mother who waved good-by to her three children by the common bush at her gate, in time to see them, all three, crushed to death by the screaming tires of a speeding car. Her comment on life and reality as it there manifested itself, a valid comment within its human limits, was to go finally and incurably insane. Is it really more plausible to see God in the confused welter of the world, where good jostles evil continually, or to see Him in the place where evil comes to sharpest focus, only to be swallowed up in the surge of the Divine love?

THE MAN IN THE MIRROR

The tradition carries at its heart the principle of its own clarification. Its complexity and confusion yields to the illumination that springs from the fact of Christ. But does this help us with the immediate problem of the understanding of ourselves?

It is helpful up to a point to notice that Christianity is part of the historical tradition and, therefore, part of the explanation of our human constitution. By this we understand, for example, why our convictions are so often stronger than the reasons we can give for them: for we are part of a living tradition which binds us to love beyond the call of reason. It is this mixed character of our inheritance, this complexity in our human constitution, which is in fact our problem. For its resolution we need some light upon our nature which will identify us to ourselves, set in proper relation our love and our reason, elucidate the true source of our obligation and give us power to perform it. Is the Christian faith more than a constituent part of a tradition, which contributes to the complexity of the tradition and therefore to our own confusion about ourselves? Or is there in it a principle of clarification, a definitive account of man's nature?

Our claim is that the true meaning of our humanity is indeed "made visible," as Karl Barth says, "in the mirror of Jesus Christ." There we have ourselves at our true valuation, and there we see ourselves, as Cromwell asks the artist to depict him, "warts and all." There we measure ourselves by our true measure, our authentic yardstick, what Paul calls "the measuring-rod of faith."[17] In this light we see light upon the meaning of our lives and the status of our reason, and the meaning of all our other parts and passions. We find that the store God sets on us exceeds any that we dare set upon ourselves, and that he holds us in his regard not by weighing our merits but by pardoning our offenses, by cherishing us not for what we are but in spite of what we are.

Already there is enough here to correct distortions in the tradition. For example, one might delineate the difference Christ made in the West by manipulating the terms *worth* and *wisdom* as they are handled in the classic and in the Christian tradition. The Greeks set much store by man's wisdom and thought little of his worth apart from his wisdom; the Christians were of two minds about man's wisdom but had no doubt about his worth, for his worth was grounded not in his wisdom but in God's love so that man's status in the love of God and therefore in the regard of man bore no relation, in Christian principle, to his sophistication. This dialectic has the most practical application, for example, to the problem of democracy. The illusion of an undistorted reason, and the notion that man's worth was inherent in his endowment of reason, meant that in the nature of the case Greek thought could produce no more than a limited democracy, in effect an aristocracy of the mind. It could not produce a government either by or for the people. It was the Christian insistence on the corruption of all men's wisdom, together with the affirmation of the equality of all men's worth, which joined with practical political prudence to give us the substantial reality of political democracy.

The same essential starting point safeguards us against false diagnoses and spurious solutions of the human problem. The "warts" on the human physiognomy which are thrown all too clearly into relief in the disconcerting mirror of Christ are not failures in philosophic or scientific or mystical *gnosis*,[18] but failures in love; they are the fundamental distortion of self-love which takes love for its healing. This is the *original*, the *primal*, sin which is thrown into sharp relief by the fact of Christ. Our prime problem is not an ignorance to be healed by any kind of pedagogy, but an introversion of the self upon the self which perverts even our piety (so that the characteristic forms of *religion* as they develop in human society and history are forms of *idolatry*, in that they propose various devices whereby the self will secure that which is valuable *for* the self) and generate the self-defeating preoccupation with the self and its concerns with which we began this chronicle.

Who, if I may be so inconsiderate as to ask, is not egocentric? . . . my slight acquaintance with pickpockets and scientists leads me to believe that they are far from being unselfcentered. . . . And so, I am convinced, are street cleaners and deaf-mutes, mothers, murderers, mountain climbers, cannibals, fairies, strong men, beautiful women, unborn babies, international spies, ghost writers, bums, executives, out and out nuts, cranks, dope-fiends, altruists (above all), obstetricians, ambulance chasers and lion-tamers.

Here e. e. cummings (quoted in some unidentifiable place by Reinhold Niebuhr) approximates an insight which is the negative element in the Gospel; but there this pervasive

94

human distemper is assaulted by a love more potent even than self-love, by the salutary serum of grace.

> [The Christian doctors] expanded the most comfortable idea of the corruption of man's nature, and the free redemption that could, body and soul, correct it.[19]

As with the understanding of man's nature, so with the vexed and vexing moral question. As opposed to the prevalent and persistent intellectual options—that moral obligation is either rationally self-validating or else a counsel of practical (scientific) prudence—Christian theology (when it knows what it is about and is not paying unnecessary deference to the philosophic or scientific attitudes) insists that Christian morality, like all morality, takes its content less from rational reflection than from personal and group loyalty. It is not in the least discomfited by being reminded that the morals of a society are socially conditioned and historically relative (after all, the word morals derives from *mores*). If man is his history, man's moral life is likely to be dependent a good deal on history too. The crucial question is: What history? If a man's life is totally bound up in his own personal history, then his "morals" will be governed by a concern for his personal welfare. If he allows himself to be cabinned and confined within the history of his own V*olk*, then his morality will be the morality of German blood or "My country . . . right or wrong." Now it is possible, it is indeed necessary, to subject these personal and parochial standards to rational scrutiny; the difficulty is that the same rational faculty which can be used to show their limitations can as easily be used to justify their claims. For reason does not of itself define human ends; it serves ends which are chosen for motives more powerful than reason. The trouble with any legislation handed down by reason, whether it be the *nous* of Plato or Kant's rational (*noumenal*) self, is that what reason prescribes reason can change; what reason legislates, reason can abrogate. Without arguing the whole case here, it is noteworthy that the classic documents of Christian faith (incorporating the classic documents of the Hebrews), while they set life in a firm and commanding frame of obligation, make no use at all either of rational or of prudential ethics. The reason is clear. They take seriously that the true *humanum* of man, that which makes him human, is not either his pure or his practical reason but his history; and the essential element of his history is his life in community. Therefore, the ground of his obligation is his profound indebtedness to the community of his nurture. This is no doubt in some sense true of every man born of woman: but the unique thing about the Hebrew-Christian understanding of the matter is that there the community of our loyalty is a communion created and sustained by the sovereign grace of the one only living and true God, a community differing both in its origin and in its understanding of itself from every other community under heaven. Any loyalty less than this, the service of God in the community of God's people; whether it be to the self itself, or to the nation for the sake of the nation, is disastrous because it is idolatrous, not because it is irrational or imprudent. Even the service of humanity may be idolatrous, since it is subject to a multitude of definitions (compare the true good of humanity as defined by the Buddha, for example, and by Marx). Christian ethics, therefore, are not rational or prudential ethics: they are the *ethos*, the *mores* of that community which has found the meaning of its life and the cement of its unity in Christ. And this is much closer to human

96

reality than are rational and philosophic ethics, or scientific ethics for that matter. If we speak to a child about responsibility, we do it not in terms of reason but in terms of loyalties: "That is simply not the way we do things." If the loyalty is real, the obligation is powerful; if there is no loyalty, there is no meaningful obligation.

If the community of obligation is a true community then the obligation is valid, within the limits of that community. But it is out of history, nurture, and community that the obligation is generated. What the Christian Gospel does is to clarify and crystallize our history, to bring us with the strong compulsion of love into the community of faith, whose loyalty is centered on Christ and which generates therefore a mesh of obligations to Him and to that human community —in principle the whole race of men—which is made of one blood and reconstituted by *His* blood.

Here, then is the fount of true self-knowledge where, to hark back to Chapter I, a man learns that he is a louse and *yet* that he can stand ten feet tall. "We are ashamed of ourselves, but we are proud of Thy love for us," say the prayers of the Iona Community.

The encounter with Christ is the supremely self-revelatory meeting. Our own estimate of ourselves is deceptive; our encounter with others tells us much, but tells us nothing final. Such encounters may be inflating or deflating for the wrong reasons; it depends on the company we keep. But in the presence of Incarnate Love there is no room for illusion: pride is burned up and pride is kindled. It is the end of self-idolatry and the birth of what the New Testament calls *the new man in Christ*. The king is dead; long live the King!

The odd thing is that the truth of Christ, which deals thus

97

finally with the problem of self-knowledge, by the same token removes the preoccupation with it. We are content to be known rather than to know. "Thou shalt love the Lord thy God, but thou shalt not know thyself." Instead of the preoccupation with the self and with self-knowledge, that frustrating and defeating introversion, there is a new preoccupation: "That I may know him, and the power of his Resurrection, and the fellowship of his sufferings, being made conformable unto his death."[20]

Earlier I quoted from Matthew Arnold:

> Resolve to be thyself, and know that he
> Who finds himself loses his misery.

There is a reply to that, not poetry at its greatest but an authentic Christian insight:

> "Who finds himself," the poet saith,
> "shall lose his misery;" ah, no!
> For long ago I found myself,
> Yet still went companied by woe . . .

> This was myself: compact of faults,
> Of failure, foolishness and sins,
> Nor could I see the end of them,
> Nor knew I where the list begins.

> Then, weary of the futile strife,
> Heart sick of bondage and defeat,
> I sought another self than mine:
> One strong enough my foes to meet; . . .

> With whom my burdened soul could leave
> Its burden of iniquity.

98

I found them all, Oh, Christ and Lord,
And lost myself in finding Thee.[21]

As poetry, it need not be defended; as Christian testimony,
it can stand.

NOTES TO CHAPTER III

1. Hick, John: *Faith and Knowledge*. Cornell University Press,
   Ithaca, 1957, p. 196.
2. Both lectures are reproduced in *The Christian Idea of Education*,
   Yale University Press, New Haven, 1957.
3. Niebuhr, H. Richard: *The Meaning of Revelation*. The Macmillan Company, New York, 1946, pp. 6off.
4. Wilhelmsen, Frederic: *History, Toynbee and the Modern Mind*.
   Modern Age, Vol. I, No. I, Summer 1957, p. 46.
5. *Ibid*.
6. Niebuhr, H. Richard: *op. cit.*, p. 77.
7. *Ibid.*, p. 80.
8. Casserley, J.V. Langmead: *The Christian in Philosophy*. Faber &
   Faber, Ltd., London, p. 235.
9. Huxley, Aldous: *The Devils of Loudun*. Harper & Brothers, New
   York, 1953, p. 17–18.
10. Williams, Charles: *The Descent of the Dove*. Living Age Books,
    New York, 1956, pp. 107–8.
11. Quoted Santillana: *The Age of Adventure*. p. 173.
12. Rupp, Gordon: *Principalities and Powers*. Abington-Cokesbury
    Press, Nashville, 1952, p. 36.
13. Most of the vexing questions, like the paradox of predestination
    and free will, can be understood in some degree by any man
    who has the experience of love beyond reason. Is the young
    man in love *free* to be in love or not to be in love? And if he
    is not free to love or not to love, is he then merely a robot? Not
    in the least. The problem is a problem only "from outside."
    He himself will tell you that he chooses to be what he cannot

99

help but be, that the bondage *is* perfection of freedom. And so essentially it is with God's grace and the response of faith.

14. What follows is to be found most usefully expanded in Niebuhr, H. Richard: *op. cit.*, pp. 109ff.

15. In addition to Niebuhr's *The Meaning of Revelation*, Casserley's *The Christian in Philosophy* has a discussion of the *singular* and the *universal* which probably does what can be done in this regard. The type of discussion with analytical philosophy (logical positivism) which is carried by John Hick's *Faith and Knowledge* promises to be even more useful.

16. Jenkins, Daniel: *Believing in God.* Westminster Press, 1956.

17. Niebuhr, H. Richard: *op. cit.*, p. 153.

18. The Gospel blessing on the *simple* are so clear as to prevent any such misunderstanding; they are indeed so emphatic that they have tempted the Church to too unqualified a distaste for learning. And it is approximately true to say that the early heresies, of the *Gnostic* type, consisted almost invariably of claims to know too much, to know more than man *can* know, to stake too much on the deliverances of *wisdom*.

19. Williams, Charles: *op.cit.*, p. 84.

20. Philippians 3: 10.

21. Evangelical Publishers, Toronto.

CHAPTER IV

Our Intellectual Age

> . . . . if the Cross is the law of life at all,
> it must be so for the intellect as well as else-
> where . . . We have to deny the premature
> affirmation which is at bottom a denial, for
> the sake of the preliminary denial which is
> an ultimate affirmation, and this is the true
> *via negativa.*
>
> H. A. HODGES[1]

I think it is true that the general thrust of the argument thus
far is in line with the movement of the times, or at least with
one influential movement of the times: from unmanageable
freedom to legitimate authority, from the thin improvisa-
tions of contemporary speculation to the "traditions of the
fathers," from the uncertainties of thought to the stabilities
of history. But before the argument be turned into sheer
archaism, there are two things to be said and said with
emphasis.

In the first place, while the character of personal being is
strongly conditioned by the past, it is not determined by it.
We recognize historical necessity not in order to capitulate

to it, but because the knowledge of that necessity is the condition of our contemporary freedom.

In the second place, the tradition itself, if we give due weight to the Christian elements in it, contains the necessary warning against the idolization of tradition.

One of the most intriguing things about the New Conservatism, conspicuous in Russell Kirk but not only there, is the confidence with which it claims the support of the Christian inheritance.

> Christianity and Judaism must always
> be conservative influences. . . .[2]

Now this has a high initial plausibility. The New Conservative emphasis upon history and tradition over against reason is at first sight congenial, since Christian faith finds the *locus* of godly illumination in history and community, and is radically critical of reason. But there is no justification in Christian theology at all for the absolutization of tradition, and Biblical religion can be made the handmaid of uncritical conservatism only by the most gross distortion.

Notice the way the Conservative argument, at least in Kirk's expression of it, runs. He is concerned to dispute the capacity of reason to order the affairs of men; in particular he challenges what he thinks of as the "Liberal" pretension—associated, for example, with Dewey—that reason riding the historic tide has the secure mastery of the future and carries an implicit guarantee of social beatitude. Against this liberal pretension of bringing the affairs of men under rational management and of measuring the human good by pragmatic tests, Kirk proposes a surer reliance upon the ancient wisdom of humanity, quoting Burke who quotes Hooker:

We admire . . . those things which are ancientest . . .[3] and speaking of

. . . the sound ancient heart of humanity.[4]

Now there is as we have said a firm base in the Christian inheritance for a radical criticism of reason: but it is quite extraordinary the ineptness with which Christian theology is used by the New Conservatism. With entire justice Kirk uses the wholesome doctrine of Original Sin to puncture a number of liberal and rationalistic illusions. He emphasizes, rightly enough, the vulnerability of reason to pride and interest, and the necessary ambiguity of all rational blueprints for the human and social future. But the doctrine of Original Sin strikes deeper than that. It makes it impossible, in the first place, to talk about "the sound ancient heart of humanity," and it blocks any notion that *any* tradition, however ancient and however sacrosanct, yields secure and final norms; for the tradition itself contains sinful elements of pride and prejudice which make it, too, subject always to criticism and to judgment. It is true that Christian theology finds *in* history its revelatory and its normative events; but history itself is not revelation, and the event of Christ *is* revelation precisely because it cuts across and calls in question men's accumulated wisdom and achievement, and shatters every historic as well as every rational pretension. In other words, while the Christian insight would teach us to take man's historic existence seriously and, therefore, to take history itself seriously as in part constitutive of man, it contains a principle of criticism both of men and of history, a principle which stands sharply against any formal conservative theory and has been recurrently the starting point of the most radical social criticism.

So much for the immediate point of the idolatry of tradition; but at the risk of digression, I want to spend a little
space in showing the dire effects of such an idolatry, and of
such an irresponsible use of Christian theology. What Kirk
is concerned to do is to sanctify the hierarchical society,
which did indeed have its historic and—less certainly—its
Christian justification in its time. But the same doctrine
which Kirk uses to qualify the pretensions of the rationalists
was used, and rightly, by Puritan Protestantism to call in
question the pretensions of every aristocracy; for every aristocracy is tempted too easily to identify its own wisdom with
the eternal law and its own interest, therefore, with the general interest. Just as it is impossible to equate the Divine
intention with the projections of men's reason (Kirk's valid
point) so it is impossible to identify the Divine intention
with any given historic order. The so-called "democratic
myth," which Kirk indicts as a purely rational concept, was
sustained at least in part by the Christian and Calvinist
recognition not only of "the exceeding sinfulness of sin," but
of the exceeding pervasiveness of sin. There is no historic
order, however venerable, which has not been perverted by
the sin of man and the pride especially of the powerful. It is
impossible to endow an aristocratic order with permanent
Christian validity because it once had provisional Christian
sanction. When Kirk goes hog-wild over the aristocratic
principle, and commends Britain because in his version of it
the working class is still "deferential"[5]—as if a deferential
working class were a sign of the Christian governance of
states—then I have to say as a Britisher that his prejudice
has blinded him to the facts, and as a Christian theologian
that his thought has slipped wholly loose from any Christian
moorings.

A democratic tradition knows what it is about when it lodges power with the people, not because it trusts the people unqualifiedly, but because it does not trust the rulers whatever their credentials. It knows enough about Original Sin to know that power is like money, which, as Francis Bacon put it,[6] is like dung—healthy only if it be widely and evenly spread.

And once Kirk's thought has slipped from sound theological control it slides into sheer rationalization of aristocratic bias. He is on safe though not on original ground when he insists on the claims of "Justice and Order and Liberty against the demand for a featureless security." It is trite but true enough to say that

> . . . there is something better than to know what it is to be guaranteed and protected and pensioned. That better state is to know what it is to be a man.

But he betrays himself and perverts Christian judgment when he goes on in high-minded fashion to declare that

> Poverty is not in itself an evil; nor inequality; nor death. All these may be occasions for virtue.

He quotes Sir Leonard Woolf's indictment of Christianity:

> Christianity envisages a framework for human society in which earthly miseries have a recognized, permanent and honorable place. They are trials sent by Heaven to test and train us; as such, it is impious to repine against them.[7]

and implies that he along with Burke would accept this impeachment. But this whole line of argument is theologically perverse. The Christian answer is, of course, that poverty, inequality, and death *are* evils in and of themselves.

THE MAN IN THE MIRROR

They are the enemies of man and the disrupters of community, to be fought with every weapon the good Lord puts into men's hands. Certainly God may pluck good out of such evils, and consistently does; but that is not a charter for tolerating them but for contending against them. "Poverty is not an evil!" It is well to be high-minded; it is better to be compassionate.

One of the most illuminating discussions of this whole matter is in Reinhold Niebuhr's *The Self and the Dramas of History*, especially in Chapter 20, "Organism and Artifact in Democratic Government." (Niebuhr is frequently claimed by Kirk and by others of the New Conservatives as one of them. But Niebuhr has too much theological gumption to fall into the pit that Kirk digs for himself.) It is no doubt true that the rationalistic liberals of the last hundred and fifty years have exaggerated the element of artifact (that is to say, the element of rational contrivance) in history and society, to the neglect of the "given" and organic. But the danger of the New Conservatism is that it will fall into precisely the opposite error, and by emphasis on the "given" diminish man's freedom and creativity. Will Herberg sets the matter in balance, and brings us back to the line of our own argument:

> Authentic religion, certainly authentic Jewish-Christian religion, can never accept the role which conservatism, in its eagerness to conserve what is indeed worth conserving, assigns to it. Religion sanctions society, but cannot be its handmaiden; it sustains the social order, to the degree that it is worth sustaining, but at the same time subjects it to radical, and what must sometimes seem shattering

106

criticism. Its standpoint can never be simply that of society itself.[8]

. . . or, for that matter, of history and culture itself, even if history and culture registered one unambiguous conclusion. Among other valid purposes which the New Conservatism serves in our day, let its aberrations stand as a warning against the idolatry of tradition, which is as disastrous as any other idolatry.

THE CHURCH'S DEBT TO HERETICS

In spite of the history of persecutions, a sensitive Christian self-consciousness has always been aware of the dangers of idolization, even of the Christian tradition itself; so much so that the phrase "the Church's debt to heretics" has become proverbial in historical theology. And it is not only true that Christianity has been saved again and again from a frozen orthodoxy by an internal and potentially heretical challenge, but it has been invigorated by attacks from without which have forced it to reassess its own claims and the grounds on which they are made.

. . . we have found it necessary in the Christian Church to accept the external views of ourselves which outsiders have set forth and to make these external histories events of spiritual significance. . . . Celsus' description of the sources of Christian belief and his criticism of miraculous supernaturalism, Gibbon's, Feuerbach's, and Kautsky's accounts of Christianity, other surveys made from the points of view of idealistic or positivistic philosophy, of Judaism or of the history of religions—these have all been events in the internal history of Christianity.[9]

One of the hazards of the present intellectual situation is that Christianity is not subject to radical challenge, so that it tends to present itself as too easy an option—intellectually too easy, that is. Of course there are pockets of resistance: in the older versions of logical empiricism, in atheistic existentialism, in mechanistic psychology and sociology; but none of these fills the role of a religious alternative, of a life-demanding and loyalty-compelling option. Not one of them has spiritual and social vitality enough to function as a "scourge of God" for the Church. A generation ago we had the advantage that to take the Christian option seriously we had to beat off the assaults of its antagonists; and this meant sharpening our own Christian understanding and tightening our Christian grip. We had to hold the line of Christian conviction while menaced by snipers like H. L. Mencken and attacked along the whole front by the massed battalions of the Marxists. And it did us, I think, nothing but good.

Mencken spent a lifetime lambasting the Church.

> A woman, a dog and a walnut tree,
> The harder you beat 'em, the better they be.

It is dubiously true of any of these, but it is certainly true of the Church . . . and Mencken knew all the language of abuse. For example:

> *Puritanism.* "The haunting fear that someone, somewhere, may be happy."

It is hardly adequate as a definition, but it is salutary as a warning.

> *Archbishop.* "A Christian ecclesiastic of a rank superior to that attained by Christ."

This is hardly just to the hierarchy, but they will be none the worse for remembering it.

If Mencken says, as he does, "If God made man, why did he make such a botch of the teeth?" one is forced to face certain difficulties in the argument from design; and one is more likely to face the issue than if someone simply suggests in a genteel manner that there are certain difficulties inherent in the argument from design.

If Mencken says, as he does, that "Rich men keep clergymen so that they may have a visible example of the fact that virtue doesn't pay," one may suspect some oversimplification, but is forced nonetheless to ask why a Church committed to identification with the poor does come so easily and so consistently under the patronage of the rich.

If Mencken says, as he does, that "What the world needs is more sin," then the sensitive reader is forced to ask what sin is and to revise his conventional notions about it, as the Bible itself would insist that we do. And his castigation of the Church was the more salutary in that, while he carefully cultivated the image of himself as an apostate and a rapscallion (he died two years ago, asking for a funeral suitable for one "irrevocably damned"), he gave us all an object lesson in some of the weightier matters of the law, justice, charity, and, in an odd way, humility; if he found himself in a post-mortem confrontation with the Apostles he would say to them frankly, "Gentlemen, I was wrong!"

We may not see his like again and, if we do not, we will be the poorer, and the Church will be the poorer. The Church would be less scandalized by atheism if it would remember that the truth of God is always obscured as much as it is illuminated by the Church's testimony; and the Church, therefore, cannot afford to be without the witness of unbelief. It is not contrary to orthodoxy to believe that God "appoints" some to be atheists as he "appoints" some to be apostles; this does not diminish the urgency of the apostolic witness (to the atheist among others) but it does check the temptation of the apostle to take himself as seriously as his message, and it does represent the care of God to keep the apostle on his apostolic toes. Think, for example, of the extraordinary danger to the university if it fell captive to an unexamined and unchallenged piety, if the Christian cause were deprived of a live opposition, if there were too many Christians and too few atheists.

A more signal debt has been owed by the Church over these last generations to a more cogent and influential heresy; and this will serve as an illustration of the fact that, since the Church has been well served by non-conformity in the past, its health depends upon an alert spirit of non-conformity in the present and the future. Clearly, of course, the most salutary encounter over the last period has been with practical and theoretical Communism. No theologian of any worth but has had to reshape his Christian formulation in the teeth of a cogent and compelling Marxist *Weltanschaung;* and the formative statements of Christian faith at this present time have a trenchancy and a relevance which would have been impossible were they not wrought out in the face of the Marxist Challenge. The marks of this encounter are on the work of men like Reinhold Niebuhr (from *Moral Man and Immoral Society* onwards) and Paul Tillich (especially in *The Protestant Era*) among the Protestants; and the notable English Jesuit Father M. C. D'Arcy recounts the same confrontation in *Communism and Christianity*.[10] On the whole it is true to say that contemporary theology simply cannot be read intelligently without some acquaintance with the Marxist outlook and terminology, so momentous has been the encounter between them. (The same is true, in another area of theological concern, of Freudianism.)

Here, in telegraphic terms, is an incomplete catalogue of debts owed by the Church to Communist heretics:

1) It has given to Christian spokesmen a salutary exercise in keeping their controversial tempers. Marxism insists on distorting a faith which is basically a matter of history and community into a version of religious speculation of the world-renouncing sort, the sort which involves an escape from history and community. One is tempted to pay back in kind and to make the worst rather than the best of the Marxist case. The discipline of learning to pay back controversial good for evil, of weighing the merits before counting the demerits of Marxism, and of realizing that the misunderstanding of the Church is largely the Church's fault—this has been a salutary exercise for Christian apologists.

2) Marxism—together with a new endeavor in Biblical studies which is itself not unrelated to the Marxist challenge —has reminded us not only of the historical and communal character of Christianity, but of the materialism of the Biblical and Christian faith: that the Bible takes the material world to be not an obstacle to spirituality but a gift of God, the instrument of his will, and the area of our obedience. Biblical spirituality, we have discovered afresh, is not a renunciation of the material, but an insistence upon its right and Godly use; an authentic expression of this use is, characteristically, social justice. The materialism which is antagonistic to Biblical spirituality is the materialism which takes the world not as a gift but as an accident. But we have as grave a quarrel with any spirituality which imagines that

God is dethroned when natural and economic law is established, as if God could work his will only by manipulation of mind and spirit. The Christian case has never rested on the assertion that spirit is triumphant over matter—as if we could shape history or master death and circumstance by our own will—but that God is triumphant over all. An economic interpretation of life is as congenial to a Christian view of man and the world as a "spiritual" one. Both have truth in them, and both need correction by a deeper perspective which makes both spirit and matter the objects of the creative and redeeming power of God. There is a materialism which degenerates into idolatry (just as there can be an idolatry of spirit, for example, in Christian Science); but the grim enemy of authentic Christianity in our day is not materialism, but the false spirituality which finds our real dependence on the material world so distasteful that it escapes from reality in an opium cloud of "religion." This kind of spirituality is especially trying when a comfortable class makes it an excuse for resisting the bread-and-butter demands of underprivileged people. "Bread for myself is a material problem; bread for my neighbour is a spiritual problem." This word of Bardyaev's has the Bible behind it.

3) The Marxist criticism of religion as the opium of the people, and of absolutist ethics as the rationalization of the interest of dominant social groups, has reminded us how often religion and ethics, including Christian religion and ethics, have functioned precisely this way.

And so one could go on: for example the new articulation of the Christian view of history, to which reference has already been made, was in large part stimulated by the extraordinary power and persuasiveness of the Marxist interpretation of history, which has in some part and in some places lost its appeal as history has uncovered new complexities. The present point is simply that the fruitful ferment in Christian theology, and the reappropriation of Biblical insights in illuminating depth, is in part due to the chastening of an emasculated Christianity at the hands of a powerful heretical movement.

The lesson from all this is that the Christian tradition is best served by those who appropriate it, not to buttress their own orthodoxy and their own intellectual security, but as a base from which to explore all the frontiers of thought. The proper role of the man who is strongly upborne by Christian conviction nourished out of the tradition is that of a *frontiersman* familiar with the far reaches of human speculation and the deep abyss of human doubt. What Daniel Jenkins says of the Christian minister is true in its measure for every Christian intellectual:

All the doubts and difficulties and terrors which confront mortal men as they face the temptations and hazards and ambiguities of existence should be his familiar ground. . . . Life at its grimmest and harshest and most enigmatic should have an almost morbid fascination for him. . . . Even if other men forget it he should have cause to know that

O the mind, mind has mountains, cliffs of fall
Frightful, sheer, no-man-fashioned,
Hold them cheap
May who ne'er hung there.

He must have all the poet's sensitivity to the unimaginable weight of the unintelligible world without the poet's saving irresponsibility.

113

One of the most disquieting features of the contemporary boom in piety is the number of those who go from undergraduate school to seminary bearing their new-found orthodoxy as if it were a personal achievement which allows them to rest on their intellectual laurels, and which carries with it an exoneration from intellectual rigor. There are the usual honorable exceptions; but all too many, in my experience, appear to turn a commitment of faith, which ought to be a charter for free inquiry, into an excuse for slovenliness in intellectual work—either because they take piety to be a substitute for thought ("God has spoken: it is no longer necessary to think.") instead of taking the service of the mind to be a prime expression of authentic piety, or because they assume that the Church is too charitable to be intellectually exacting, or (and this is in some cases not too severe) they are simply "weak sisters" who have fled the chill winds that blow across the world of thought to a sheltered, cloistered, and, therefore, spurious "belief." This dismal phenomenon is not inexplicable: it may be that when the normal spurs to intellectual and academic endeavor—among them personal and professional ambition—are dulled by the Gospel, when, if you like, the devils of pride and ambition are expelled or at least partly overcome, you have a house swept and garnished to be at once invaded by normal human sloth and slovenliness. Piety brings its own spiritual perils. There is a saying among the Roman Catholic clergy, "The nearer the altar the farther from Christ," which registers the conviction that a cosy familiarity with Divine things may be as menacing to the soul as exclusion from them, that Christ is best to be found on the frontiers and in the desolate places of human life, where thought is tested and faith is tried.

"The foxes have holes and the birds of the air have nests, but the Son of Man hath not where to lay his head" . . . The frontier is a dangerous, unsettled and uncomfortable place, but [the Christian] must force himself to live there and, like John the Baptist, never allow himself to be soothed and enervated by the wines and bake-meats of the city but content himself with locusts and wild honey.[12]

THE FRONTIER SITUATION

The intellectual frontier at this present time is an exhilarating place to live. These may not be times to try men's souls as do times of more obvious stress and strain, but this is a time to try men's minds; and if our earlier assertion be true that a man finds his true stature and the meaning of his life in challenge and encounter rather than in introspection, there is much to be discovered, at least about the intellectual stature of the self, simply by stepping out into the intellectual arena.

In the first place the frontier situation is generating a new cultural endeavor, in particular a new literature of penetration and of depth. As the Noble Lecturer for last year says in one of his books:

We are confronted on all sides with a spiritual ferment, an existential wrestling, an exploration of ultimate issues.[13]

It is

. . . as if the membrane between man and the spiritual world had grown tissue-thin, or had even been broken, and strange new powers were at work in the world.[14]

Men are being forced to deny all "premature affirmations":

Man in this world is in a situation that always quietly, sometimes traumatically, batters him from beginning to end. His life in solitude and among his fellows is a dizzy process of construction, demolition, construction again. He thinks he understands, and then he is pounded by data which demolish his understanding, and has to build a deeper, broader-based one. He thinks he knows what the drama of human life means, but this knowledge is secure only within small patterns of experience. His experience becomes wider and wilder, his protective comprehensiveness, his order-making patterns are pulverized—and he's off again on a new construction . . . Art flourishes with vigor both when there is a consensus about a provisional meaning (as at the time of Queen Elizabeth in England) and when the inrolling tides of meaninglessness threaten to engulf (as in our own time). . . .

Art penetrates in order to establish truth, shatters in order on solider ground again to build, cracks categories in order to dramatize the mercurial truth of things that will not be at home in a cognitive house.[15]

True it is that one cognitive house after another has come down; one intellectual God after another has failed. It is not surprising that on the one hand the air is filled with what Karl Barth calls "existential screaming," while on the other hand some men retreat to firm if somewhat barren ground and patiently begin again the building of a house of the mind, using only words which can be made to do duty as mathematical symbols. The Christian who has passed even a part of the living tradition through his own mind will have the feeling that he has heard much of this before; but for the sake of the contemporary brethren for whom Christ died, he must go through it again, not simply as a matter of intellectual comprehension but as a matter of the profoundest participation. At all costs he must avoid "the tendency to enjoy, cheerfully and unctuously, the race's bad health," of which Kathleen Nott accuses the contemporary orthodox. He may have his own conviction that he knows of "solider ground on which again to build"; but he can make that conviction contagious and persuasive only if he himself goes through the deep waters of existential doubt, and even pays entirely serious attention to the contention of his "positivist" colleagues that all the most poignant questions are meaningless because they do not have an answer out of scientific reason. And if some men begin to believe, as they do, that "the locus of the soul is neither in London nor in Vienna, but at the barred gate of Eden,"[16] then the Christian can welcome them home there with understanding only if he himself has known the sting of exile, and how strongly barred those same gates are.

The strength of the Christian cause in our day is that it is finding spokesmen who have themselves gone the long way around to find themselves at home in the Christian tradition, and who, therefore, conversely, are so firmly grounded in that tradition and the conviction that it carries that they can move freely on the intellectual frontier.

One of the most fascinating features of the contemporary university situation, for example, might be described this way. The universities (I speak particularly of the faculties) are full of good humanists who are only one generation away from a Christian upbringing. In my own university sons of parsons are thick on the ground. But they were either brought up in so conservative a mold that they had to revolt from it for the sake of their intellectual freedom and integrity;

or they were brought up as liberals (or modernists, in terms of the fundamentalist-modernist controversy) so that they made the transition to humanism without noticing that they had done so. As part of their scholarly and intellectual equipment they have a good knowledge of the great tradition, including the Christian elements in it; but my impression is that they have never considered Christianity as a live and contemporary option, competent to throw light upon the deep problems of the mind and the deep dilemmas of contemporary life. It is only over the last years that they have begun to notice that it is the Christians who appear to dredge up out of the tradition insights profoundly illuminating upon the most topical of questions. I think that on the whole it is Paul Tillich who has done this for the philosophers and psychologists, while Reinhold Niebuhr has filled the same role for the social scientists, especially perhaps the historians. I am not suggesting, for I have not noticed, a stampede into the Church on the part of the literate humanists; they still with fair accord reject what is for them the public image of contemporary Christianity. But Tillich and Niebuhr simply stand symbolic of the fact that for multitudes of devoted intellectuals Christianity, which had been a cultural and historical, even antiquarian, interest, now presents itself as a commanding alternative for the life of the mind.

Short of a digest of the contemporary cultural conversation, which is out of the question, let me simply indicate one or two of the chief points of interest, and then illustrate the nature of the present situation by reference to one specific issue.

1) CHRISTIAN ANTHROPOLOGY AND
DEPTH PSYCHOLOGY

Part of the reason for the present preoccupation with the self is, no doubt, that modern psychology has put into men's hands all kinds of new equipment for a fresh attack on the intransigent problem of the self. Insofar as the analytical study of the psyche—its anatomy and pathology—is a part of self-understanding, as indeed it is, we are immeasurably better equipped than were our predecessors for this quite vital work. It may be a piece of special pleading, but from the present perspective it does appear that the deeper the analysis of the psychic self is driven—from Freud's naturalistic and highly individualistic version, to Adler's recognition of volition[21] as well as biologic drives, to Jung's insistence on the importance of the social and historical factors, to the still more synthetic approach of the so-called Vienna Circle—the closer the conjunction appears, not necessarily between the conclusions of depth psychology and Christian anthropology (*anthropology* used here as that department of theology which concerns itself with the doctrine of man), but between the range of questions with which the two disciplines are bound to concern themselves. I speak as a fool in this area; but is it misleading to say that the effect of Jung's psychiatric work is to insist that "to be a self is to have a history" and the effect of Caruso's work is "to be a self is to have a God"? Neither can determine what a man will make of his complex history or determine Who is "the one only living and true God," for these are decisions of faith; but a Christian anthropology, which at least tries to deal with man in his wholeness and his history, can talk more easily with a psychology which disguises neither man's wholeness nor his history than it can with a truncated version of man's nature.[17]

2) THE SIGNIFICANCE OF THE PUBLIC EVENT

Logical positivism (logical empiricism, analytical philosophy) initially, as in Ayer's *Language, Truth and Logic,* characterized theological propositions as literally nonsensical, conceiving them to have the character of speculation, and as being subject to no possibility of empirical verification or denial. The whole situation along this front is now highly fluid. On the one hand Ayer's original position has been subject to radical qualification, by Ayer himself in the Introduction to the 1946 edition of his work,[18] and by other logicians who are indebted to his work but disassociate themselves from his conclusions. On the other hand theology has been increasingly meticulous in extricating itself from any confusion with metaphysical speculation, and more and more recognizes that its essential methodology is the explication of the meaning of public and historic events. Insofar as theology recovers its own proper starting point and method, and logical positivism interests itself in history as well as in science and mathematics, there would appear to be a convergence, or at least a possibility of fruitful discussion. This whole process has gone further in Britain, where theology had a shorter road to travel to get back to its proper business than it has in this country. The whole discussion promises to be immensely helpful as it is adumbrated in *New Essays in Philosophical Theology,* which is edited by a theologian and an analytical philosopher, and which represents the initiation of a debate which is bound to draw in those who care about precision of language and of thought and who care particularly to analyze the logical (epistemological) status of theological language. The discussion already has served two positive purposes: in the first place, it makes it no longer necessary, but rather archaic, for theologians and logicians to shout at one another, as if the former were proposing fanciful answers to meaningless questions and the latter refusing to formulate any except semantic questions; in the second place, the sharp edge of logical analysis is helping to shear the theologian away from his chronic temptation to confuse his own work with the work of the speculative philosopher, and to free him for his proper business, which is the exposition of Holy Scripture and the articulation of the meaning of the events to which Scripture bears witness.

In addition to *New Essays in Philosophical Theology*[19], we also have John Hick's *Faith and Knowledge*, of which some use has already been made. Both books are invaluable in making available in America the results of the British debate thus far; reference is made to the later work of Wittgenstein (the father of the analytical movement) in criticism of strict positivism, a work which is made readily available and is developed in an original fashion in the writings of John Wisdom of Cambridge.

These are two areas only in which the contemporary conversation between Christianity and culture is increasing both in intensity and depth; the issues in each area are exacting enough to enable us to sharpen our Christian wits, and deep-going enough to illuminate our human situation. There are similar frontier situations in every area of intellectual interest: of history, of law, of the social and physical sciences, of education and the arts. Each has its developing literature, and in each there are exhilarating discoveries to report. Since theology knows better than to make the old claim in the old form to be "Queen of the Sciences," its interest in the frontier territory is not to establish itself with any kind of royal authority: it simply asks for room to witness—rather as did the Church of the American frontier—that, as the scout opens up the territory, as the prospector assesses its resources and the engineer subdues it to human purposes, it is God's world they are exploring, it is the gifts of God that they are "exploiting," and it is the children of God for whom the new land must be made habitable.

THE WHOLENESS OF MAN

The encounter between Christianity and culture comes, of course, to its sharpest issue on the question which is closest to our present concern: the identification, dissection, and location of the human person.

I have referred already to the protest against mechanism and scientism eloquently argued in Joseph Wood Krutch's *The Measure of Man*. Here is one of the greatest of the old-line humanists doing battle against those who would deny the validity of man's incorrigible conviction of freedom and responsibility. His indignation is not only against the theoretical inadequacies of those who would describe man as wholly manipulable, and subject to the designs of the "human engineers." More menacing than the overt utterances of the academics, which are alarming enough, is the seeping into the minds of non-academic men of the conviction that human life is subject to the same necessities as is the subject matter of the physical sciences, and so subject to the same controls. This mood would be menacing, Mr. Krutch argues, even if its presuppositions were correct. For even the assumption that man is wholly manipulable, whether it be true or false, contributes to the destruction of manhood. If it is true, it is knowledge that we cannot afford, for even the illusion of freedom is better than its denial.

The presuppositions of the human scientists would be fatal if they were true; but they are of course not true. It is not to be denied that man is subject to biologic and psychic and social conditioning, but to run this through into a denial of freedom and responsible rationality is a manifestly self-contradictory procedure. For the perception that man is a conditioned being is itself a rational perception.

> How . . . can the consciousness be dismissed as an epiphenomenon when only by virtue of this epiphenomenon could it be perceived to be an epiphenomenon—or anything else.[20]

He might have gone further, as does Paul Tillich in the recent volume of his *Systematic Theology*,[21] and referred not to the perception but to the *conviction* that man is a mechanism. What is the status of this conviction? Is it simply that the mechanism is set in a particular way? What would be the response of the honest mechanist if he were challenged to give up his conviction that man has no freedom; to give it up, say, or suffer martyrdom? Is the question meaningless; and, if it is not meaningless, is the denial of freedom itself more than an empty and meaningless form of words?

The Christian difficulty with Krutch's argument, even while we welcome his doughty assistance against the mechanists, is that while he recognizes the limited usefulness of demanding responsibility from men who don't believe that they are free, he is not able to acknowledge that man's problem is *in* his freedom. He will have men see that their very humanness is in their freedom, but he does not apparently himself see that whatever appeal the mechanists have lies precisely in the fact that the freedom which is part of man's essence is also his burden and his problem. His polemic against the human engineers is a humane service, and at this point the Christians have in him an eloquent ally, along with all men who cherish their humanity and are unready to renounce it. But he has not actually taken the measure of man, either in his dignity or in his wretchedness. And so he is reduced to believing that the alternative to renouncing our humanity is simply to assert it. He has not heard or will not credit that it is our very humanity—the dimension of our freedom—that constitutes our problem. "Bare" freedom is insupportable, so insupportable, as Albert Camus and many another has pointed out, that its assertion is always the preliminary to its surrender, for example, to the collective reason as in Rousseau and in Marx. The only question is whether to put ourselves in bondage to "the beggarly elements of the world," that is, surrender our manhood to something less than man; or to surrender to that Greater than man in Whom manhood is enhanced and emancipated, in Whose service is perfect freedom. "Either the true God or an idol." The Christian affirmation is that there *is* an alternative to the renunciation of our humanity: its renovation by the love of God. But that is not a *human* possibility, nor a humanist option.

One may take Krutch's diagnosis of the human constitution to be a sort of *horizontal* analysis in terms of the *levels* of man's being. He will not have it that the full story of man's life can be told in mechanistic-biologic terms. There is the reality of reason, and of rational transcendence over biologic necessity. The dimension that he misses is that level of self-transcendence, including transcendence over reason, which opens the question of man's relation to a Self above the self which is the subject matter of theology.

There are other diagnoses of the human constitution which proceed in a different way, if you like in a *vertical* way. They open up again in contemporary terms the old *naturalistic, rationalistic,* and *romantic* alternatives.

An interesting example lies to hand. One of the publishing sensations of the last years was Colin Wilson's *The Outsider.*[22] It is an odd piece of philosophic and literary virtuosity, not as good as its first patrons would have had us believe, and not as bad as Mr. Wilson himself claimed he thought it, after the storms of criticism beat about his head. It has flashes of sheer brilliance in the midst of the muddle. In the chapter called "The Attempt to Gain Control" he has an extraordinarily acute analysis (within certain limits) of three representative "outsiders" of the last couple of generations: *T. E. Lawrence, Van Gogh,* and *Nijinsky,* each dedicated after his fashion to the finding of his humanity, though they sought it along very different roads.

Lawrence was the modern Stoic, who would by will make reason supreme over passion, and unify his existence in the power of a self-consistent *idea.*

. . . all my life, objects have been gladder to me than persons, and ideas than objects.

"I could not approve creation," because creation includes a welter of vitalities which are intransigent to reason. And because the pure idea cannot have the mastery of the world and of the passions, he commits in the end of the day a kind of suicide of the mind, renouncing the self which he had falsely equated with reason, the self which "could not stop thinking" and yet could bring its thought to no conclusion—renouncing it for a life of sheer sensation, the brute sensation of killing speed. And so he died, hurling his motorcycle into a hedge at seventy miles an hour.

Van Gogh followed another road. With him, it is no longer a discipline of the intellect; his powers of will were directed to the development of the emotions. Rather than master the vitalities of the world by the sheer potency of reason, he will *love* the world and all its vitalities with the force of a most passionate nature. But the world cannot be loved indiscriminately; emotion that runs riot is emotion that rides roughshod over every relationship that ministers to the true necessities of the self. The love that has missed its true Object runs out in a torrent of indifferent adoration which has in it no reciprocity, no grace. And since love without an Object which is also a Subject leaves the life empty, the end is the bullet in the belly and the last words: "Misery will never end. . . ."

In Wilson's account of the matter Nijinsky embodies one further option:

I am feeling through flesh, and not through the intellect.

The aspiration here is after an organism perfectly attuned to the voluptuous vitalities of the world: "I am insight through flesh, not through either mind or feeling." The dance represents "the rhythmic, Dionysian upsurge of the vital energies," not subdued to reason but disciplined by athletic expertness to yield the utmost of pure sensation. But this paradise of pure sensation was invaded from other, demanding levels of the self: a moving human compassion for the victims of the

time and of the war, the nagging obligations of a marriage
which disturbed the pure animal balance. He fled this in-
vasion "into a world of his own," ever farther from the
realities of the human world. "On Good Friday, 1950, he
died at last in a London institution, still in a mental twilight."

Lawrence's problem is that "he is never alive in what he
does," he never feels what he thinks. He could write, "I
am insight through mind, not through feeling." Van Gogh
could write: "I am insight through feeling, not through
mind." It is Nijinsky who can say "I am insight through
flesh, not through either mind or feeling."

One is bound to recall Montaigne:

Into how many parts have they divided the soul? . . .
They have the power granted them to rip, place, displace,
piece and stuff it, every one according to his own fancy,
and yet to this day they possess it not.[23]

Surely the point is that the self cannot "possess" itself, still
less shut itself up within the limits of mind or emotion or
organism. The self, as the Biblical and Christian faith has
always taught, is boundlessly open beyond all the limits of
thought and feeling and sensation; it is open to the other and
to the divine Other who alone can unite all its parts and
passions in an integrating loyalty which curiously binds without constricting. In the end of his strange book Colin Wilson confesses indebtedness to Reinhold Niebuhr, that master
Christian analyst of the nature and the destiny of man. But
what Wilson actually does throughout the book is to delineate what happens to the man who takes the human problem
seriously, and tries to handle it unsuccored by Christian
insight and by Christly grace. What such a man does is to

127

select one of the human options and follow it to its logical limit; and that way, Wilson summarily says, madness lies, and death. Most of us are "saved" after a fashion, it would seem, by our lack of radical seriousness—or by the unremembered grace of heaven.

NOTES TO CHAPTER IV

1. Quoted Daniel T. Jenkins: *The Gift of Ministry*. Faber & Faber, Ltd., London, 1947, p. 65.
2. Kirk, Russell: *The Conservative Mind*. Henry Regnery Company, Chicago, 1953, p. 432.
3. *Ibid.*, p. 33.
4. *Ibid.*, p. 36.
5. *Ibid.*, p. 423.
6. Catlin, *The Story of the Political Philosophers*. Tudor Publishing Company, New York, 1939, p. 227.
7. Kirk: *op. cit.*, p. 31.
8. Herberg, Will: *The Commonweal*. Sept. 9, 1955.
9. Niebuhr, H. Richard: *The Meaning of Revelation*. The Macmillan Company, New York, 1946, p. 85.
10. D'Arcy, M. C: *Communism and Christianity*. Penguin Books, 1956.
11. Jenkins: *op. cit.*, p. 66. (What a caricature of the apostolic office is the common public image of the Christian minister. I recall that in New Zealand the National Railways advertised their service under the slogan SAFETY, COMFORT, ECONOMY; their poster represented *comfort* by a businessman, *economy* by a Scotsman, and *safety*— Heaven preserve and forgive us all!— by a minister!)
12. *Ibid.*, p. 65. (The reference again is specifically to the minister, but the point is valid for any Christian intellectual who takes his calling seriously.)
13. Wilder, Amos: *Modern Poetry and the Christian Tradition*.

Charles Scribner's Sons, New York, 1952, p. xiii.

14. *Ibid.*, p. 210.
15. Sittler, Joseph: *On Christianity and Art*, The Student World, No. 2, 1955.
16. Wilder: *op. cit.*, p. 212.
17. There is a growing literature on this frontier, a literature so considerable that any listing is bound to be highly selective. Systematic discussions are in Roberts: *Psychotherapy and the Christian View of Man*. (Charles Scribner's Sons, New York, 1950. Outler: *Psychotherapy and the Christian Message*. (Harper & Brothers, New York, 1954.) A great deal of the work of Paul Tillich is pervaded by this concern, and Reinhold Niebuhr's *The Self and the Dramas of History*, together with essays by Niebuhr and Herberg in *Freud and the 20th Century* (Meridian Books, 1957) spells out a theological comment on the matter.
18. Ayer: *Language, Truth and Logic*. Dover Publications, Inc., New York.
19. Published in the USA by The Macmillan Company, New York, 1955.
20. Krutch, Joseph Wood: *The Measure of Man*. Bobbs-Merrill Company, Indianapolis, 1953, p. 122.
21. Tillich, Paul: *Systematic Theology*. II. *Existence and the Christ*. Chicago University of Chicago Press, Chicago, 1957.
22. Published in the USA by Houghton Mifflin Company, Boston, 1956.
23. Above p.

CHAPTER V

Our Contemporary Age

From thinking us all soul, neglecting thus
Our mutual duties, Lord, deliver us.
JOHN DONNE, from *The Litany*

When we moved out of tradition and into the contemporary world we did not indeed move out of tradition; for it is central to the argument that the man who thinks and lives in the contemporary world is inseparable from his history and inexplicable without "the story of his life," which includes the history of his culture. What we *have* recognized is that the story of our life goes on, that the man who is his history also makes his history, and that the forces—for example the intellectual forces—which beat upon the world beat also upon each man. It is better that we face them freely than that we be battered by them insensibly, either into base conformity or into pointless reaction.

We measure the stature of our soul by wrestling with the currents of our time; and we come near to the full stature of our soul when we wrestle with the currents of our time, not in order that the character of our own life be illuminated, but that truth itself be established. There is such a thing as conversion in the life of the mind, wherein we are delivered by the truth itself from seeking truth for ourselves, the truth that feeds our prejudice, and we are set free to seek the truth that shines in its own light. There is a cross in the life of the mind, whereon is crucified the premature affirmation which is itself a denial. Those are the great moments in the academic community when the usual intellectual posing and posturing which affects both faculty and students is abandoned under the irresistible compulsion of the truth itself. Men are most themselves, intellectually, when they are least concerned about what kind of a figure they are cutting, either in exhibition of their own wisdom or in defense of their own prejudice. These are the rare and lovely moments, when truth itself has its way with us, and under its pure compulsion our poor defenses go down. They are like the drawing back of the gate of the intellectual Eden, before men's reason was corrupted into ideology, and men's minds made captive to pride and fear. At this point the resources which stem out of the Christian faith are of vast help to us; for if a man's worth is not measured by his wisdom, and if our status in the love of God is not dependent on our cleverness, then we are freed from any compulsion to kid ourselves about our wisdom or to pretend we are more clever than we are.

Intellectually, then, we are most ourselves in those thoughts which are least our own, in which the self-consciousness of our own intellectual processes is swallowed up in the strong compulsion of the truth itself. But the same is true at every level of our being; we are most ourselves in those acts which are least our own, which are done not out of any compulsion arising from within, but under a compulsion which

is put upon us from without, and which is obeyed spontane-
ously and without self-consciousness. This is the character
of love, which is the character of life.

It is at this point that we have to call most seriously in
question that preoccupation with self-analysis with which I
began. If it be true that the self is constituted chiefly by
history and community, then the elucidation of the meaning
of life will be in pretty direct proportion to our participation
in the issues of history and the concerns of community. The
Bible and tradition alike declare this to be true—that man is
essentially not a natural man or a rational man but a *Covenant* man, who is most himself when he is incorporated into
the community, and least himself when he is cut off from it
in a preoccupation with the self, with the self's concerns, with
the self's salvation. *Salvation* in the Biblical and Christian
meaning of the word (in Wycliffe's Bible it is consistently
translated *health*) means precisely to be extricated from the
self's sinful preoccupation with the self, and to be incorporated into the Community which is the fruit of Christ's self-
offering.

This means, according to the consistent teaching of tradition, two things:

In the first place, it means *the Church*, not an ideal
Church, but "warts and all," with all its sins on its head.
Extra ecclesiam nulla salus (no salvation outside the
Church) is not a Romish notion, as some Protestants falsely
imagine, but a Reformation commonplace. It means, against
all individualism and unchurchly mysticism in religion, that
redemption is incorporation, that man is nearer to God
when he is nearer to his human brethren. In the Church
are provided for our health what I have elsewhere called
"the merciful mechanisms of grace"[1] by which the self is

emancipated from itself, delivered, that is to say, by a new set of human and divine preoccupations from its boring preoccupation with itself. No self is ever delivered from itself by a simple determination to be selfless; such a resolve simply gives a new foothold for pride. (Like the Indian sage who visited us recently, who always self-consciously spoke of himself in the third person to show how unself-conscious he was!) And it is not so delivered, either, by a *philosophy* of self-transcendence. For the self is not in bondage to a false *idea* which can be driven out by a stronger idea of selflessness. The self is a complex bundle of lusts and drives which in the natural man are organized around a personal center which is, in any Christian reading of the matter, a false and idolatrous center. The *ego*-centricity which is man's natural constitution is in fact *ec*-centricity, a distortion of the Divine intention and of authentic human nature. If this false and phony, this literally damnable organization of the self is to be broken up, it must be broken by forces stronger than its own idolatrous principle and totally reconstituted. The process of redemption is like the shifting and reordering of a magnetic field, where by the sweet compulsion of Christ the human and resistant particles are drawn into their true relation to Him and to one another.

This is the true meaning of "the Church on the corner." Of course its essential life as a reconstitution of the body of mankind according to its true and living Principle is obscured by all kinds of sinful and sociological factors. It is a shadow of its authentic self. But there is no place else on earth where the truth of the human and social constitution is bodied forth, as it is here in Word and Sacrament and Community. It is by the strain and stress of wrestling with the intransigent self, in the commitment to live in community with other

134

intransigent selves, that there are discovered at once the need of grace and the power of grace, which is to say simply the need and the power of love.

In the second place, the social self which is the true self comes to its full stature not simply in the Church, though the main lessons must be learned there, but in profound participation in all the concerns of men. "Religion is politics and politics is brotherhood," said William Blake, and though the phrasing is unorthodox the point is sound. The grace which both illuminates and empowers the self, which lights up the meaning of its existence and enables it to fulfill the meaning of its existence, is let loose in our lives in the measure in which we ask for it; and to ask for it means to place ourselves in the exposed place where there is need for it, which is the place of *human* need.

I risk a short installment of autobiography at this point. I came to Christian maturity—or at least to adulthood—in the end of the twenties and the beginning of the thirties, a period characterized by these two things. First, at that time Christianity as we understood it was primarily a matter of social activism. Jesus was the pioneer of a new and more co-operative social order, the Gospels were acceptable only insofar as they delineated the spirit and method by which that new order was to be brought in; Paul and his successors were notable not for any contributions they had made, but rather for their success in diverting the original revolutionary impulse of the Gospel into a dead end of dogmatism and ecclesiasticism. There is practically not a word of truth in this, as we now see, but that was the way it looked to us then. Second, in the years between the wars the social issues, from our vantage point, seemed to have simplified themselves to two: war, and the competitive order which caused war. So we were, quite simply and almost to a man (and this, by the way, was true of liberal and radical Christians not only in faraway New Zealand but in this country) pacifists and socialists. Towards the end of the twenties, therefore, I spent a good deal of my time before the magistrates as a result of refusal to perform military service. I wasn't dealt with with any particular rigor, but the memory of those days is pretty vivid. In the early thirties the issues had shifted, and now those of us who were of that mind were preoccupied with the dire results of depression. I recall riots in all our cities, marching endlessly with unemployed men demanding bread for their families, long nights of conference with bitter men on the edge of open violence. Many of my contemporaries went Communist. I did not; and I am not to this day sure how far that was due to Christian farsightedness, how far to plain timidity. But I have small patience with those contemporary men who boast that they came through those years without so much as getting their coat singed by Communist teaching. Where in the world were they? Because in my experience Communism *at that point*—with forty million unemployed in the major industrial countries of the West—offered not only the most cogent theory but the costliest and most impressive practice of any social movement; and the dire and terrible logic of its idolatry of history had not become obvious, at least to us.

I would not now defend any of the positions I then would have died for—at least not in that form. I hope that this is due to deeper insight and not simply to increasing debility. Of two things, in any event, I am certain. In the first place, I don't regret the ideological errors of those times. I am quite satisfied to have been honestly in error and to chalk it up to experience. What I do regret are the times when I failed to meet a challenge because the ~~risk~~ was too great, or to meet a need because the ~~cost~~ was too great. I don't regret any of the times I stuck my neck out for what I then thought right; I do regret the times I kept it in. And that leads to the second thing of which I'm sure: that even out of the now-lamented failures in courage and in compassion there was something to be gained, and something indeed was gained. I learned from what we then did and from what we failed to do; I learned what was in ~~man~~ of compassion and of cowardice—and I learned what ~~was~~ in me. I learned, for example, that my readiness to accept the role of a locally notorious pacifist was in part due to a sincere devotion to the Gospel as I understood it, and in part quite certainly due to a ~~liking~~ for the ~~role~~ itself. And while we paid a price for our identification with unemployed workers, I doubt if we were free, and certainly I was not free, from the "I thank Thee, Lord, that I am not ~~as~~ other men are—indifferent. . . . conservative. . . ."

Now I don't know where else could have been secured that somewhat humiliating self-understanding, certainly not out of a classroom discussion on the Christian doctrine of human nature and human weakness. It had to be wrought out of an actual exposure of the vulnerable self to the pressures of the time and the complexities of the social struggle.

As things are now, I think that the situation is more complex and more difficult. For one thing we are not now tormented, most of us, by the actual and visible presence of blatant injustice. For another, even those who are undergraduates have lived with the distant rumor of dire and terrible wrongs until their capacity for response has atrophied. We know that six million Jews died in the Hitler horror; the fact is unimaginable, and yet it diminishes the urgency of lesser wrongs. Edna St. Vincent Millay laments the wilting of elemental compassion, and her eloquence can teach us of the compassion we have lost and of the compassion we want to feel, especially those of us who profess to be Christians:

> A thousand screams the heavens smote;
> And every scream tore through my throat.
> No hurt I did not feel, no death
> That was not mine; mine each last breath
> That, crying, met an answering cry
> From the compassion that was I.

Here is the profound compassion for the communities of men which we know to be our human constitution, and from which we know ourselves shut out. It is not only that the nerve endings of our compassion have been cauterized by recurrent wrong beyond our capacity for feeling or for action, but that there seems no sure way by which we can strike a blow even against the offenses which are evident, and the woes which still afflict the world.

The second disadvantage under which we now labor is that issues which then seemed simple have become desperately complex. The notion that the dwindling of the pacifist group is due to weakening of the Christian fiber is only partly plausible; it is due also to an increase in Christian sophistication about the realities of power. And the fact that many Christians who were socialists a generation ago are socialists no longer has to do with a more literate understanding not only of capitalism's power to reform itself, but also of the dangers of the unification of political and economic power. We are confronted with no simple options, but with an immensely complex society about whose mechanisms the best-informed specialists differ, a society so intricate that it seems impossible to get one's hand on the controls, a topsy-turvy world in which the old simplicities have been over-turned. George MacLeod of Iona tells of a journey he made in North India some years ago. He saw in a railroad station a wooden crate labeled for shipment, and marked, THIS CASE SHOULD BE CARRIED BOTTOM UPWARD. So far so good; but it was further labeled, THE *top* IS MARKED *bottom* TO AVOID CONFUSION. The problem is, then, where to take hold. And it is small wonder that when it seems hard to gain a pur-chase on events men retreat from responsibility and that we all have the impulse simply *cultiver nos jardins*. It is no accident that in America, coincident with this sense of the futility of public activity, an unprecedented number of gar-dens are cultivated with unprecedented energy.

Stephen Scott in *Christianity and Society*[2] said an interest-ing thing about the late Senator Joe McCarthy:

> There was a certain pathos about the battle of liberals against Joe McCarthy. We fought him so hard not simply because we were alarmed by this threat to democracy, but because this was a battle that could be understood un-ambiguously in terms of liberalism's traditional categories. It was a sort of recess from the age of the cobalt bomb and the lonely crowd.

I think that many of us have a certain nostalgia for McCarthyism—as an enemy that is; it looked like an evil thing located in an evil man, a fit target for uncomplicated indignation and uninhibited action.

But over most of the field the old terms socialism and capitalism, liberalism and conservatism, no longer define for us, as once they did, what the Communists would call "the front of struggle." The issues now are more subtle, the battle more confused. Generally, I suppose it is true that the liberal cause has triumphed all along the front, but in the process the fighting has grown more muddled. Some positions need to be consolidated, some exposed units need to be pulled back. Over most of the field the even lines have been dissolved into a general melee. It is no longer easy to distinguish friend from foe; sometimes it is easy to persuade ourselves, fighting local skirmishes alone and surrounded, that the ground we are on is not worth holding. We long for the old days—again I speak nostalgically—when the base was in sight, and the banners, when we knew what we fought for and loved what we knew. The temptation now, with confused warfare all about us and no certainty as to how the battle goes, is to dive for the thicket or slide into the ditch of our private and professional preoccupations. Many one-time warriors *have* found their private ditch and can neither be pleaded nor prodded out of it. There are remnant cries of "Forward," but they fall on deaf ears since neither those who cry nor those who hear are sure which way *is* forward. To drop the awkward military metaphor, it is small wonder that the impetus to social and political activity has withered on the vine, and that we have an absorption in personal analysis and private concerns.

And even allowing for the remaining urgency, for example of racial problems in this land, and the fact that still, even in the midst of what we think of as general prosperity, nearly half the population is short of the decent means of subsistence, we have the feeling that the domestic social problem is on the way to a solution, that we have the built-in legal and political and economic mechanisms for its solution. The citadels of injustice are beleaguered and soon to fall, or so we feel, and it would be gratuitous to go crusading against what is manifestly a lost cause. Even if it be argued, as it is very eloquently argued by George MacLeod in *Only One Way Left,*[3] that we have simply "exported our proletariat" so that we live by the labor of exploited workers in Saudi Arabia and southeast Asia, and that the incidence of injustice is as great as ever if we hold to the notion of one world; yet it is infinitely more difficult to hold in compassionate imagination the dire need of the peasants of Asia than it was to muster indignation about the visible necessities of the dispossessed of our own nation.

CHRISTIAN DEMANDS AND RESOURCES

Two things the Christian faith and tradition do for us in the midst of these very real perplexities and distresses:

1) The circle of concern which is drawn by the Gospel is as wide as the world, and it is not permitted us to contract the reach and range of our compassion. It is humanly inevitable; it is Christianly forbidden. It is humanly impossible to make vivid to our imagination the needy multitudes of unknown men; but to let it be determinative of our duty is the impossible possibility to which we are called as Christians. For in the solidarity of Christ the most distant man is as dear as any man, and all men are as near as the nearest and dearest. Humanly speaking this is a piece of blatant nonsense; but we are speaking not humanly, but Christianly; and by this judgment we are all in jeopardy, and our sins of omission weigh us to the ground. At this present time, 50 per cent of the world population takes 9 per cent of the world's income; we belong to the 50 per cent that takes the remaining 91 per cent. On the concrete meaning of this I

141

shall speak in a moment; but *for* the moment it is enough to mark the rigor of the Gospel's demand.

2) We are troubled not only by the remoteness of the need, but by the complexity of the time. Decisions which once seemed clear-cut have become precarious; and it is very difficult to bring to the precarious decision the seriousness and faithfulness which we pride ourselves that we bring—and often do bring—to life's major and clear-cut options. Yet it is the character of Christian faith to dignify the most precarious decision as it dignifies the remotest man. Our natural impulse is to feel that when a decision—about war, or political allegiance—may so easily be wrong, that very fact exonerates us from taking it too seriously. We have seen how this robs our generation of political and social commitment. Yet it is to this very point that the Christian faith speaks most cogently. I have not in this book done much about the elaboration of specific Christian doctrines. But the central doctrine of the Reformation, the doctrine of *justification by faith* (which is part of the common heritage of Christendom, and no invention of the Reformers), is a prime resource in the sphere of conduct, especially when Christian decision is bedeviled by the impossibility of complete certainty in moral and social judgment. Luther's great text: "The just shall live by his faith," actually stands in the original (Habakkuk 2:4), "The just shall live by his faithfulness." The depth of its meaning both here and in Paul is unfathomable, but it means, among other things, two things. It means in the first place that we are answerable not for the accuracy of our conclusions, but for the integrity of our choices. We are bound to act faithfully; we are not bound to act correctly. It means in the second place that in the mystery of the Divine economy our faithful choices, even if they should turn out to be

empirically mistaken—if, that is, we can look back one day and decide that we weighed the facts poorly, or that we got the facts wrong—are overruled and deflected by the Divine wisdom to serve the Divine purpose and the human good. The sum of the matter is that in the context of this living faith we are held to a close integrity, even in the midst of our dubiety, about choices from which other men turn away; it means that we can make the precarious decision with a high seriousness yet with a certain nonchalance—or at least without onerous, vexing, and crippling anxiety.

THE CHURCH IN THE WORLD

The contemporary shape of the Holy War is quite desperately confused, and yet it is by participation in the Holy War that we find ourselves and become ourselves. Though we are not always clear which way is forward, we are not reduced to running round in circles, for there are certain constancies in human life in spite of its tumult, and certain constancies in the shape of the Church's conflict against death and the Devil. W. A. Viseer 't Hooft put it somewhere that the task of the Christian now as always is to prove that the Church exists. It is put even better, I think, in the Westminster Confession of Faith, which speaks not, as is so common, about a visible and invisible Church, but about *one* Church which is "sometimes more and sometimes less visible." The task of the Christian, in those terms, is to make the true Church visible. We are all concerned that the lines of the true Church are blurred if not obliterated by social compromise, by racial discrimination and the like. The problem here is real and urgent; but it is not the whole problem. For the nature of the Church is not primarily social and political, but organic and evangelical. If the true form of the Church, including its true social and racial form, is to be recovered, it must be recovered *whole*. That is, our social-political concerns are safely handled only in the context of a more comprehensive concern—the concern, as the informal motto of the ecumenical movement has it, "that the Church be the Church."

It is only in a Church that is true to itself that our human life is illuminated; and yet, paradoxically, we are to seek the true good of the Church not in order that our human life may be illuminated, but because it is the will of God that the race be incorporated into Christ.

We can delineate the true form of the Church under four aspects, and then concern ourselves particularly with the last two:

1) *Worship*. Much of our Protestant worship is simply not *edifying*. It has neither true Catholicity nor true contemporaneity. It is shapeless, superficial, sentimental, subjective. And *edifying* worship is, as in derivation the word means, a worship which *builds up* the Christian body by nourishing it out of its source. It is directed not to religious self-expression, which is a highly unruly business, but to the glory of God—and to *glorify* God, as some of the translations clearly put it, is to *clarify* God, to "*make known* His ways to the children of men." It tells us the meaning of our lives by telling us the story of our lives in the dialectic of self and grace; it lights up the meaning of our history by making it an episode in that long salvation-history by which God is finding and shaping a people for Himself. In Baptism it declares that before men are white or black or rich or poor or bright or dumb they are equally sons of the most high God, and by the *washing* of Baptism it affirms that we come to that high

destiny not by any momentum generated out of our own life, but by the grace generated in the love of God and mediated in the Community of the faithful. In Holy Communion it speaks of a solidarity which is grounded not in kinship or in interest, but in "the love wherewith Christ has loved us." By recalling us continually to the meaning of Christ's death, it teaches us to care infinitely for man's life.

To perform all this, worship has to be cleared of sentimentalism and grounded firmly in Scripture and tradition. Its essential elements deal not with religious aspiration but with Divine activity. It is perverted when it becomes subject to individual and pious caprice, either of minister or people. Especially in the University community but not only there, those who hold responsibility for the life of the Church owe to the community a worship which in form and substance is governed by the great inheritance and not by the whims and poor insights of "those who simply happen to be walking about." This is not a hindrance to the "liberty of prophesying" for which our New England fathers were prepared to die; it is the condition of all authentic prophecy. For by liberty of prophesying we do not mean the rule of whim and fancy in religion, but the strong articulation in contemporary terms of the faith once delivered to the saints.

2) *Doctrine.* We have at Stanford University an old and odd provision that in the University Church Christianity is to be presented "without doctrine." It is a little difficult to see how Christianity can be taught without "teaching," which is the simple meaning of *doctrina;* and since we don't know what the provision can mean in practice we don't let it worry us overmuch. I suppose it was really designed to exclude *divisive* doctrine; but I think it probably reflects an earlier and still prevalent notion that *doctrine,* and more

145

especially *dogma,* is the enemy of spontaneity and vitality in matters of faith. And so indeed it can be. I have referred already to a somewhat infantile orthodoxy which can be the enemy and sometimes the end of free inquiry. But when orthodoxy functions this way it has ceased to be *right teaching* (*ortho-doxa*) and becomes wrong teaching. For the emancipating truth of the Gospel, which it is the business of Christian doctrine to set out, emancipates among other things from the fears that affect the mind, from the fearful clinging to old truth because it is old, from the fearful fleeing from new truth because it is new.

If the Church, then, is to enter fully into the freedom where with Christ has set us free, it needs the liberating truth and it needs to have it set out in order. The preacher does violence to the congregation if he reduces the vast and varied proclamation of the Scriptures—which speak in due place and due proportion of salvation and of society, of justification and of justice, of piety and of poverty—to the poor limits of his own insight.

One of the most exhilarating aspects of the current religious revival, among much that is depressing, is the fact that it goes along with a theological revival in which it is being discovered again that the half-truths of contemporary naturalism and existentialism, for example, are both contained and transcended in the Scriptures and in the great dogmas based on the Scriptures. To appropriate Scripture and Tradition is not to fall victim to a false bibliolatry or a frozen and inhibiting orthodoxy, but to find our prisoned thoughts take wings, and to find the perplexing riddles of our own nature yield to a Truth which clearly knows us better than we know ourselves.

3) *Discipline.* This is an unfashionable word which has

meant much historically. Etymologically it has the same root as *discipleship*; but by usage it refers to the pattern of life of the believing community, the way in which it orders its life to clarify and exemplify the faith by which it lives, and the love by which it is bound. One of the most bewildering things about contemporary Protestantism is its apparent capacity to make do and to grow without any very recognizable discipline of life. The lesson of history would seem to be that the survival of a community over the long haul depends in essential part upon symbolic and behavioral patterns which identify it to itself, seal its members' identification with it, and dramatize the meaning of its life to the outside world. Most commentators on Judaism, for example, would relate its stability through the generations to its ritual and ceremonial life; and clearly one of the reasons for the appeal of Roman Catholicism is that it proposes a discipline, devotional, penitential, and moral, which will pull a disorderly and undisciplined life into some kind of *shape*. Every normal human and historical probability would argue that a Protestantism which is shapeless in worship and imposes no rule of life will not take any significant strain over any significant period; but prophecy is dangerous and not our present business, and there are in any event signs that contemporary Protestantism is recovering its classic roots and a relevant modern form.

The point now is that we have to begin to fill in the outline at least of a Christian discipline which is true to the Gospel and applicable to the times. The Gospel not only illuminates the long sweep of human history and the broad map of our times, it throws into high relief what William Blake called "the minute particulars" of our personal behavior. "Mind well," said he, "the minute particulars." It is not possible to serve Christ in the large and neglect the details. Of course by detail I do not mean the picayune negativisms about smoking and the like which make the poor substance of so much Protestant discipline; I mean that the life of the Church must mirror the faith of the Church, and the life of each member of the Church must declare in act as well as in word that he has passed from death into life because he loves the brethren. And to love the brethren is a concrete and exacting business, whose cost we ought to weigh. "Love in action," said Dostoevsky, "is a harsh and terrible thing compared with love in dreams."

The test point here is *money*. You may protest that for most of us, especially those who are students, the commodity is not plentiful enough to be embarrassing. Let's concede that for the moment; but that is simply an argument for thinking the matter through while we are free from the blinding bondage of possessions. And it has to be thought through, for there is no point at which the practice of the contemporary Church more sharply denies its profession than at the point of economic behavior. I know that in an overspiritual generation it may seem sordid and unedifying to discuss money and the way we get and spend it; but if you take the long tradition, there is probably no subject with which Christian teachers have been more preoccupied than with the relation between piety and possessions—and more specifically with the relation between piety and poverty. "Gold and the gospel never did agree: religion always sides with poverty."[4] The Church has always known that as the love of money is the root of all evil, so the use of money is the best test of virtue.

I recall one of the meetings of the Amsterdam Conference of Christian Youth in 1939. The Conference had ruled against applause, on the general grounds that not all speakers were equally understood in a multilingual group, and it did not want to discriminate between them. The rule was well kept. Then one day we heard from Pastor Elie Lauriol of France, a virtually unknown and unspectacular figure, who spoke out of the midst of the needs of French workers, and spoke of the need for a profound identification with contemporary men. He outlined the conditions of contemporary usefulness, and ended: "Il n'y a rien à faire avec l'homme qui n'a pas vaincu *d'or!*" The predominantly English-speaking crowd of young people took a moment to catch the meaning in translation: "There is nothing one can do with the man who has not conquered *gold!*" and then the hall cracked with their cheering. They knew as we all know that one prime enemy of our obedience is our unreadiness to surrender the chance of pampering the self which is represented by ample cash in hand. Our own reluctance to think radically here is buttressed by the sense that the issue is irrelevant: for do we not have in America a way of economic life whose genius it is that one man can get rich without impoverishing another? And is it not true that in the strange complexity of the times America's high standard of living is a benediction to the rest of mankind? An offense, maybe, but a blessing nonetheless, since a myriad economics float on America's bounty—and her purchasing power? There is substance in all this; but what then are we to do with the consistent witness of the tradition that "man is made for hardness," that wealth is always a threat to authentic piety, and that the rich man is excluded from the kingdom of God (save for a special miracle: the camel and the needle's eye) because his wealth bars him from real solidarity with his brother man?

Probably none of the traditional answers will match our

contemporary need. "Tithing," which is being widely recommended and less widely practiced, is irrelevant in an unequal society: the man who tithes $20,000.00 a year can get by tidily on the remaining $18,000.00; the man who tithes $5,000.00 may find it hard to get by at all on the remaining $4,500.00 The monastic solution has always been limited, though its appeal continues in the rigid Catholic pattern and in a variety of Protestant variations: John Wesley's "get all you can, save all you can, give all you can" is too uncritical of the way in which the money is *got*. I lived for some years in a British group whose accepted discipline was to keep their personal and family expenditure on a level—the national average income—which in rough justice seemed to be their share, to pool the rest and give it away where it would do the most human and Christian good. Don't tell me that wouldn't work: it worked very happily for ten years, until the group, which was largely professional, became largely underprivileged! But I am not proposing a solution at this present time; I don't know what the solution is in a country with such vast diversities of privilege as this one, and such varied costs of living. The average family income over the whole country is something under $4,000.00; in my own particular area it is over $6,000.00 (with a corresponding cost of living), while there are large areas of the country where it is under $2,000.00 and goes often much lower than that. But even if the solution be obscure, it is clear that those who care for the Church's integrity cannot be content with a situation in which the Church reflects every disparity of privilege in the world outside, and in which we put all our souls in jeopardy by an unexamined economic practice which is a practical denial of our solidarity with the needy of the earth.

Two things seem to be called for:

150

1) As we work out the meaning of our own Christian commitment, it should include, as every authentic Christian commitment always has included, an undertaking not to enrich ourselves by our professional craft, but to accept it that whatever financial rewards come our way, we will hold our personal standard of life to that simple level which will enable us to perform our personal and professional responsibility efficiently, and also enable us to free the maximum amount of money for the good cause and for the needs of men. This kind of basic commitment to a decent simplicity of life is not only a matter of simple obligation in a world still half hungry; it is a good deal less fussy than petty rules of life touching drinking, smoking, and the like. If the major decision is made the others pretty much make themselves. And such a decision is emancipating in respect to the choice of vocation itself; for it means that when life is firmly set upon an abiding commitment to simplicity, job choices can be made on their merits, and the cash consideration can be subordinated as it ought to be.

2) With all patience and realism, we need to find over the next generation the kind of corporate discipline in economic matters which can guide individuals and groups who are beginning more and more to see that this neglect of economic brotherhood is a prime failure of the Church in our day. I conceive that a Church community which is increasingly serious about its commitment, and uneasy about sustaining a Church committed to Christian rigor by shows of the late fall fashions, might respond eagerly and with a strong sense of release to a discipline which would emancipate us from the competitive social pressures, give some edge to a Christian challenge to Exurbia, and a positive reason for avoiding the new car each year. The requirements of such a

discipline are that it avoid romanticism, involve no playing around with monasticism, and bear some relation to the actualities of economic brotherhood in a world of vast and sinful disparities of wealth.

3) *Outreach.* In the areas of Worship, Doctrine, and Discipline we are concerned simply that the Church be true to itself, that it glorify God in its corporate body, that it prove that the Church exists. But the limits of the Church's concern are not set by the limits of the Church community; and there is no area of social life where problems of human urgency are not of Christian concern. That is commonplace enough, but to take it seriously brings enough hard work for any lifetime. Work for the mind, first of all: to bring the faith into some relation to the facts of life; and the even more exacting business of making our life match our understanding.

> Knowledge we ask not, knowledge thou has lent,
> But, Lord, the deed, there lies our bitter need,
> Give us to build above the deep intent,
> The deed, the deed.[5]

As intellectuals (our calling, not our pretension) our special business is with ideas, and our special temptation to make ideas a substitute for action instead of the means to action.

There are several areas presently requiring the best of our Christian dedication both in mind and act.

Vocation. We inherit a doctrine of Christian vocation which is full of illumination. It stems from Scripture but has its most influential expression in Luther. It sanctifies the common and material life by making it the arena of holiness, and it sanctifies every useful mental and manual craft, measuring the worth of it by its plain utility. There is no space here to spell it out,[6] but the situation at the moment is that a great deal of the doctrinal and historical material that we need has been recovered and is available. There are two general problems which need more and better thought than they have been given. In the first place, we are moving into a period when the brunt of the world's work will be borne by machines, and the bulk of the human factor, if not its relative importance, will be diminished. A nice balance needs to be kept here. As long as it is necessary that what Aristotle called "servile work"—that is, work for the mere sustenance of the individual and the human community—be done by human hands, it must in any Christian reading of the matter be thought of as a mutual ministry, as dignified as any work to which men put their powers. But it is dignified by its usefulness, and it ceases to be dignified as soon as it ceases to be useful. What happens to *men* when the machines pick up the weight of the work? The present assumption, both of owners and unions, appears to be that they must be kept at work, since they must have income both as livelihood and as purchasing power; and we have never contemplated paying men except for work—except when we pay them for investment capital. Are men displaced by machines to have work made for them, or are they to be paid for work they don't do or don't need to do, or are they to have an owner's share in the machines and the product flowing from them? And insofar as this problem is solved, and men are freed from sustenance work for what we now call *leisure,* is this to be a source of frustration or an opportunity for that other mutual ministry of cultural (what Aristotle called *liberal*) work? The questions are large, and in one sense they are new; but they stem out of the tradition. They are unavoidable when the inherited faith touches the contemporary fact. We shall not get much further with them until they are picked up from the theologian and carried by those who in the professions and in industry bear the heat and burden of the working day. And that burden is lessening by the year, so that the work remaining and the leisure that is growing need both to be understood in Christian terms.

The main outreach of the Church into the corporate life of men is through Christian men who know their Christian business there. It will take all the theological acumen, the practical penetration, and the personal and corporate devotion of the generation that is now finding its way to Christ.

Politics. I hope that we are now seeing the third stage of a dialectic process. Time was—we have referred to that time —when the Christian fashion was to put too much stake in political activity, as if we could devise a political practice which was the secular application of the Gospel. When the provisional and precarious character of all political procedures became all too clear, we had the present reversion to a concern with the personal and interior life. As the classical Christian inheritance has been progressively recorded over these last years, we have learned to consolidate our political responsibility while moderating our political expectations:

> Realism can be a very good thing: it all depends whether it means the abandonment of high ideals or of foolish expectations.[7]

It is quite a trick in political matters to keep our ideals without overdoing our expectations. I think that the trick is beginning to be learned, partly by the long work of Reinhold Niebuhr and those who have learned from him. A sample of the practical political wisdom which is beginning to be generated out of the theological revival is in William Muehl's

Politics for Christians,[8] an invaluable handbook for the working Christian politician.

I am avoiding here any detailed discussion of particular issues, even the most exacting of all: the problem of war and contemporary war making, and the problem of race and race relations. I avoid them here because they cannot be handled here; but there is no avoiding them in thought and practice. And there are other issues which need more attention than they get. We are living at the moment, for example, in reaction against a late version of Puritan Protestantism which elevated teetotalism almost to a Scriptural absolute, which it is not. But in San Francisco one out of every six adults is a problem drinker or a full-blown alcoholic, and this is simply the extreme of a nation-wide problem. Christian duty at this point is not discharged by the happy-go-lucky and mildly alcoholic demonstration that *we* are not puritans. Call it if you like simply one of the "minute particulars" that William Blake insists we "mind well"; but it is also a neglected and complicated area of social responsibility. And in the light of recent findings, it would seem that the personal use and the social role of tobacco constitutes another.

I have been concerned not to solve problems, but to demonstrate that insofar as our problem of personal self-understanding depends on social participation, we need not lack areas of activity. We were busy in earlier chapters with the role of tradition, and especially with the crucial role of the Christian inheritance if we are to make sense of our existence by making sense of our history. But orthodoxy in idea, while it may illuminate, cannot justify our existence. It can be wedded to the grossest neglect of those concrete obligations by which our soul is stretched to its Christian size; there are

155

Christian communities in South Africa and in the American South which are impeccably orthodox after their fashion— where the Bible is enthroned and even, curiously, read— but where orthodoxy is matched with grim and cruel social tyranny. We all know how easily such a split can grow; for every one of us has to live with his private version of it.

Only love is the fulfilling of the law, the perfection of every orthodoxy, and the white cloak that will cover a multitude of heresies. Sound doctrine will help us to avoid all kinds of pitfalls in theory and practice; but the worth of our piety is to be measured, not by our skepticism about false solutions, but by our service to right causes. So we have to be our contemporary age as well as our Christian age; and we cannot come to anything like our Christian stature except under the stress and strain of contemporary life and contemporary need.

I give you, finally, a quotation from an unlikely but for me a favorite source. Shortly before he died Damon Runyon reviewed his own last book, *Short Takes*, and wrote as follows:

> Damon Runyon, in a simulation of humor, often manages to say things which, if said in a serious tone, might be erased because he is not supposed to say things like that. By saying things with a half-boob air . . . he gets ideas out of his system on the wrongs of the world which indicate that he must have been a great rebel at heart but lacked moral courage. I tell you Runyon has subtlety but it is the considered opinion of this reviewer that it is a great pity the guy did not remain a rebel out-and-out, even at the cost of a good position at the feed-trough.

No man knows what his neck is worth till, at least once,

he has stuck it out with the chance of having it chopped off; and no man knows what his life is worth, or even what it means, until he has learned to risk it. From the Christian point of view, we are not vainly summoned to "stand on our own two feet;" what we are called upon to do is to put to the contemporary test a faith which comes to us as the most vital part of our inheritance, which we share with the Church of the ages and to which our deepest selves respond.

NOTES TO CHAPTER V

1. Miller. *The Renewal of Man*. Doubleday & Company, Inc., New York, 1955, p. 180.
2. *Christianity and Society*, Summer issue, 1955.
3. MacLeod, George: *Only One Way Left*. Published by the Iona Community, Glasgow and Edinburgh.
4. Herbert, George: *The Church Militant*. (Herbert is here voicing what over the centuries is virtually a Christian commonplace.)
5. John Drinkwater.
6. There is a growing literature on the matter. Probably the best recent discussion of it is in *Work and Vocation* (John Oliver Nelson, Editor), Harper & Brothers, New York, 1954, and there may be some remaining usefulness in *Christian Faith and My Job*, by the present writer, published in New York by the Association Press, 1946.
7. Martin Wight in *Looking Forward*. Royal Institute of International Affairs, London, 1946. Quoted in *The People Shall Judge*: University of Chicago Press, Chicago, 1949, Vol. II, p. 808.
8. Muehl, William: *Politics For Christians*. Association Press, New York, 1956.

CHAPTER VI

Selfhood and Salvation

> It is certainly the part of a Christian man to ascend higher than merely to seek and secure the salvation of his own soul.
>
> John Calvin[1]
>
> Only those go to heaven who are willing not to go.
>
> CORNELIUS LOEW on *Luther*[2]

The argument thus far is a kind of extended commentary on the saying of Jesus that "He that findeth his life shall lose it, and he that loseth his life (for my sake) shall find it" (Matthew 10:39): shall find it, I think it is true to the Gospel to say, both in the sense of understanding it, and of appropriating it. The self's question, "Who am I?" is a question which the self cannot answer, since the self does not live in and for itself; the answer has to be *given*.

George MacLeod tells the following pathetic story out of the war:

At an army boxing tournament in France, between two

159

bouts, they led round the ring a soldier from hospital who had lost his memory. The hope was that from the Army Corps of spectators with whom he had served one man at least might recognize him, and so assist his cure. None however did. As the man, frustrated, was led down from the ring he threw out his arms and cried, "Will nobody tell me who I am?"[3]

Notice, first, that he had lost his identity because he had lost his *memory*; the story of his life had been blanked out. He could be reunited with his past, and therefore with himself, only if he could meet up with someone who could tell him the true story of his life, give him a history and so give him a self. This is in analogy the reference to tradition with which we were concerned in Chapters II and III.

> History is the stuff of life, and any inquiry into the meaning of life becomes, at some stage, an inquiry into the meaning of that ongoing process of life, individual and collective, which we call history.[4]

Man does not understand himself by identifying those processes of nature in which his life is grounded (the characteristic view of heathenism, and of modern naturalism, e.g., Marxism) nor does he "come to himself" by extricating some timeless substantial self *from* the processes of nature (the characteristic Greco-Oriental view: Atman *equals* Brahman). He knows who he is and he comes to himself (as in the story of the *Prodigal Son*) when he recalls the true story of his life. This is what Jaspers means when he says:

> Where I belong, and what I am living for, I first learned in the mirror of history. For a Western man this story is partly told in the Western inheritance, but for no man is it ever

fully told till he discerns in it the loving activity of God in creation and redemption which is the theme of the Christian story, and the inner meaning of all men's lives.

The conviction that man stands too completely outside of both nature and reason to understand himself completely in terms of either without misunderstanding himself, belongs to general revelation in the sense that any astute analysis of the human situation must lead to it. But if a man lacks a further revelation of the divine he will also misunderstand himself when he seeks to escape the conditions of nature and reason. He will end by seeking absorption in a divine reality which is at once all and nothing. To understand himself truly means to begin with a faith that he is understood from beyond himself, that he is known and loved of God.[5]

He can know this only because the story of his life includes tokens and signs of the love of God, of which the chief and most unmistakable is Jesus Christ. The mirror of nature is opaque, the mirrors of mind and of history are distorted. Said Pascal:

Scepticism is true, for after all, men before Jesus Christ did not know where they were, or whether they were great or small.

"Man is the creature made visible in the mirror of Jesus Christ."

THE DEATH OF THE SELF THE BEGINNING OF SELFHOOD

The shape of the self is given in its history, but it is still a self and not simply a history. It transcends its history; it is "boundlessly open," in Buber's phrase, to the multiplicity of life in the world; and in particular, since it is shaped finally *by* love and made finally *for* love, to the exhilarating demands of the Divine and human Other. The story of its life goes on, contemporary style. It is most itself in those thoughts which are least its own, which are thought under the compulsion of objective truth; and in those acts which are least its own, which are performed under the compulsion of love. The merit of scientific work, when it is pursued short of idolatry, is that it is conditioned by this submission of the self to the fact, so that it generates its own quality of disinterestedness and its own distinctive virtues. The same is true in the sphere of action: In his *Leaves from the Notebook of a Tamed Cynic* (written in the twenties), Reinhold Niebuhr drew an interesting contrast between Detroit (the scene of his parish activities) and Los Angeles (which he chanced to be visiting) in terms of a contrast between extroversion and introversion.

Perhaps Detroit is typical of the America which works feverishly to get what it wants, while Los Angeles is typical of the America which has secured what it wants. On the whole I prefer the former to the latter. An honest enthusiasm even for inadequate ends is better than a vacuous existence from which even the charm of an imperfect ambition has departed. Of course the paganism of power is more dangerous than the paganism of pleasure, but from the perspective of a mere observer it is more interesting. Who would not prefer Napoleon to his imbecile brothers who merely luxuriated in the prosperity created by his ambition?[6]

162

The comment is dated, since the West Coast is booming in the fifties as Detroit was booming in the twenties. But we still have the signs of enervation, along with the noise. In any event, Detroit, in Niebuhr's impression of it, was too busy with the pursuit of inadequate ends to have time for introspection; Los Angeles luxuriated in introspection, and generated a welter of exotic cults out of a hothouse preoccupation with the self and its meaning. The self, he seems to say, is truer to itself when it has some God outside the self, even when that God is a false God, than when it makes a god out of the self. The very definition of psychosis is a self wholly oriented around itself—where the world means nothing except a threat to the self. "How much larger your life would be if your self could become smaller," says G. K. Chesterton. "Alice must become small if she is to be Alice in Wonderland."[7]

Both in the life of the mind and in the life of action venturesomeness pays dividends and timidity pays none. The mariners of Bremen justified their dangerous voyaging with the motto:

Seafaring is necessary—living is not necessary.

And we know in our bones, that in this sense a willingness to accept death is the condition of fullness of life. The mind which is afraid of new thought is the mind progressively incapable of any thought; the life which is never risked is the life which is never lived.

"Give us security," we ask of life.

"And would you then have death before you die?"

Hear Chesterton again:

"He that will lose his life, the same shall save it," is not a

163

piece of mysticism for saints and heroes. It is a piece of everyday advice for sailors or mountaineers. It might be printed in an Alpine guide or a drill book. This paradox is the whole principle of courage; even of quite earthly or quite brutal courage. A man cut off by the sea may save his life if he will risk it on the precipice. He can only get away from death by continually stepping within an inch of it. A soldier surrounded by enemies, if he is to cut a way out, needs to combine a strong desire for living with a strange carelessness about dying. He must seek his life in a spirit of furious indifference to it; he must desire life like water and yet drink death like wine.[8]

We all know that this is so and testify to it by our private sense of deprivation because the times make life so easy for us, and by our private envy of the students on the Budapest barricades. This can be romantic, even neurotic, like the early Christian mania for martyrdom. What we have to do is to launch out into the hazardous deep that is in our minds and in our world—into the frontier areas of thought and action where the law is "Nothing ventured, nothing won."

What the Christian faith does is to attach a strange promise to our venturing: that we shall find no area of exploration which lies beyond the garrisoning of grace, that the Divine resources are precisely matched to our need. "The sea is the open hand of my Saviour." But this we cannot know in advance; it is only when we make the leap, either into intellectual or into personal jeopardy, that we verify the fact that we do not leap into the void. When we do make it, leaving the self-defeating preoccupation with the self's knowledge of itself and the self's realization of itself, we find that it is in the costly encounters, where the mind's certainties and the self's securities are put in jeopardy, that the high affirmations of the Gospel "speak to our condition."

. . . in interpreting our present, we use the life and death of Christ as a parable and an analogy. The scribes and Pharisees now sit in Peter's seat, and in the Churches of St. Paul priests plot defence against the disturber of the people; disciples are corrupted by thirty pieces of silver; money-changers and those who sell human victims for vain sacrifices conspire with Pilates who wash their bloody hands in public; poor unreasoning soldiers commit sins which are not their own; betrayals and denials take place in every capital; and lo, out of cumulative self-deceit and treachery, out of great ignorance, out of false fears and all the evil imaginations of the heart, crosses are constructed not for thieves but for the sons of God. We see . . . how bodies are now being broken for our sake and for the remission of sins the blood of innocents is being shed. . . . We learn to know what we are doing and what is being done to us—how by the infinite suffering of the eternal victim we are condemned and forgiven at the same time; how an infinite loyalty refuses to abandon us either to evil or to nothingness, but works at our salvation with a tenacity we are tempted to deplore.[9]

And, as we have seen, the assurance of faith, the initial confidence which justifies the adventure of mind and act, the confidence that the frontier of thought and life is a place not of desolation but of grace—this initial confidence is generated not out of private ecstasy but out of the public proclamation of the Gospel, and out of the community of faith which has grounded its common life there through these many generations. For the Church when it entered into the open secret of the Gospel, says Charles Williams, "ecstasy was no longer specially to be desired, for the ordinary daylight was as much He as the extraordinary night."[10] "We find our heaven on foot," not be going along with any spiritual elite if such there be, but by plodding in the ranks of the pack-laden, mud-bogged infantry of the Gospel, who have no mystic insight, but whose meat it is to do His will.

> Look at the generations of old, and see:
> Did ever any trust in the Lord and was confounded?[11]

So far, then, our discussion has brought us. Now I want to break out of the main frame of the argument and speak more generally about the meaning of the Christian faith for our life and for our time. And since these chapters are addressed in the first instance to a university audience, I shall refer somewhat directly to the problems of the college community, though they are problems pretty characteristic of society in general.

I have been around and about on the American campus now for upwards of ten years; and it will not be out of order now if I react positively, even violently, to the religious and intellectual situation as I at least have seen it.

I confess that I am bound to think the incorrigible individualism of the times is the source of most bedevilment in matters of faith. It is compensated for, but not corrected, by endless joining; it is not corrected because on the whole the joining is done to cover an anxious individualism, and for "what can be got out of" the group. It is, I suppose, a characteristic of fallen human nature; but it is enhanced by the American ethos. The world is my oyster; and everything that is proposed to me, including education and religion, is to be tested by whether or not it helps me open it. I have referred

166

elsewhere[12] to a questionnaire sent out by an influential Christian group which asked, "What do you expect to get out of religion?" A multitude of students gave their answers —but no one apparently took exception to the question. Yet it is as true of religion as it is of education that we get nothing out of it till we stop asking what we can get out of it; but that involves a pretty complete inversion of what we think of as normal human behavior. It is precisely such an inversion that Christianity proposes, with its talk of the new birth and the new man. "Christianity is the deepest hurt that can be inflicted upon a man," as Kierkegaard says, because it batters remorselessly at the very citadel of the self, and will promise nothing to the man who will not yield it up.

Nowhere is the enthronement of the self's individuality more clearly manifest than in the area of religion. Religion is to give: whether it be to give me a secure set of values, or to give meaning and significance to my life, or, in a more evangelical variation of the heresy, to give me personal salvation. There are, it is worth noting, no words in the Bible which can be translated either value or meaning or significance, because the concern of the Bible is with something else. The Bible does speak about salvation; but, as we have seen, the central Biblical meaning is deliverance from the self, including the self's anxieties about itself and its salvation.

The extraordinary appeal of the Oriental redemption religions probably stems from this root of chronic individualism. Nothing confuses counsel in matters of faith like the amiable suggestion that Asian piety is simply another, probably more spiritual, version of the faith of the Gospel. It is probably more spiritual, in one possible meaning of the word; but that, from the Christian point of view, is the trouble with it. Actually about the only thing the Buddhist and the Christian have in common is their common humanity. That is a good deal, but they have it also in common with the Communist and the atheist. In matters of faith, as Will Herberg says, what one affirms the other denies.[13] The characteristic of Asian mysticism—I am inclined to say of all mysticism, except where it is more Christian than mystical—is that it proposes to relieve us of the embarrassment of selfhood, either by transcending it or by obliterating it.

The mystics supposed that if I completely immerse myself in myself there opens up, as it were, a pit within me into which I can sink down until I come to the bottom where I am identical with all beings.[14]

Whether this identity with the All of Being is the fulfillment or the obliteration of selfhood is always obscure; but either way the aspiration is away from the involvement of the self with other individual selves, in a costly mutuality whose demands can be met only by the renovation—not the obliteration—of the self. "The Christian would rather be saved in Christ than lost in God," said James Denney (I don't know where). I am not sure that "to be saved in Christ" is more humanly appealing than to be lost in God, but in any event it is of such a salvation that the Bible speaks. It proposes to deliver us from concern about the self, even about the self's salvation, by generating in us, under the impulse of the love of God, a love *for* God and for the brethren which consumes self-love and with it the concern for self-fulfillment. The paradigm of it is St. Paul's "I could wish myself accursed from Christ for my brethren" (Romans 9:3).

If it were possible empirically to prove the inspiration of the Hebrew scriptures, it might be by demonstrating the

extraordinarily sure-footed way in which the Bible avoids
even any flirting with the perennial philosophy or with
mysticism. So alluring is that piety which proposes a transcendence of time and history and absorption in timeless
Being that it is almost impossible to understand how the
Bible *could* avoid it were it not for some providential over-
ruling. And yet the Bible does avoid what is, outside the
Biblical tradition, almost coincidental with human reflection;
there is no talk of values, no talk of Being, no promise of self-
realization except as the paradoxical fruit of self-abandon not
to Being but to Love. "Seek first the kingdom of God," which
is often made the justification for a thrust *beyond* the world,
is in actuality a summons to disinterested action *within* the
world: for in context it reads, "Seek first the kingdom of God
and his *justice*." "The kingdom of God is *within* you" should
read more accurately, "The kingdom of God is *among* you."
The emphasis is constantly sociological rather than psychological, public and corporate rather than inward and individual. For the Bible is concerned with something other
than the soul's aspiration: It is concerned with the work of
God and the role of the people of God—and with the desper-
ate plight of those men who by the idolatry of the self and its
concerns shut themselves up in loveless isolation from the
Community of Faith and Love. And even when the Scriptures have a mystical sound—as when St. Paul talks of being
"in Christ"—the reference is not to extrication from the
world and absorption in Being, but to extrication from self
and incorporation in the Body of Christ—into the company,
that is, of His people.

Of course the self has a worth and a status, but it is not a
worth which it has for itself, but a worth which it has for
God; and it is not a status which it cherishes for itself, but a

status which is bestowed on it by God. Bernard of Clairvaux, in his treatise *On the Love of God* discriminates four stages of love which represent the sequence, not in time but in the logic of love, of the Christian life. The paraphrase is desperately inadequate,[15] but the argument goes somewhat like this: The natural man by the nature of his human (which is to say his fallen) constitution loves himself chiefly; this is the first stage of love. But this same natural man in the mercy of God is called away from the single love of self; he is gifted with blessings and beset with troubles which draw him out of his self-sufficiency, and turn him toward God as a source of his blessings and a refuge from his distresses. This man is religious. He loves God, "but still for a while for his own sake, not for Himself;" he loves God for the gifts that He gives and for the succor that He promises (this is the second stage), "but is it not true that even though the breast were of steel or the heart of stone in one so many times rescued, it must of necessity be softened by the grace of the Redeemer so that man might love God not for his own sake but for God Himself." This is the third stage of love, when a man no longer loves himself simply, nor God for the sake of the self, but God for His own sake. It is only in the fourth stage that the self is mysteriously restored, not now as having value in itself but "for the sake of God," and for the service which the self can do to God. Of course the whole inner dynamic of faith, which is the logic of love, is destroyed if the self is offered *in order to* be restored: "For not without reward is God loved, although He should not be loved for the sake of the reward."

The whole tradition is suffused with the understanding of this paradox of self, and the dialectic of self and love. The poets of course do better with it than the theologians, except when the theologians, like Luther, are poets themselves. But here it is in the poetic tradition, in Richard Crashaw's *Against Irresolution:*

> Yield to His siege, wise soul, and see
> Your triumph in His victory.
> Disband dull fears, give faith the day:
> To save your life, kill your delay.
> 'Tis cowardice that keeps this field;
> And want of courage not to yield.
> Yield then, O yield, that love may win
> The Fort at last, and let Life in.
> Yield quickly, lest perhaps you prove
> Death's prey before the prize of love.
> This fort of your fair self, if't be not won,
> He is repulsed indeed, but you're undone.

SOME NECESSARY QUESTIONS

This transmutation of selfhood has its effect on everything men do: on their eating and their sleeping, joying and sorrowing, loving and sinning, their living and their dying. In one sense things are less simple, since the dimensions of reason and nature are cut across by the line of the Divine love. Reason is dignified, but there can be no simple confidence in it; nature is to be enjoyed, but not with the uncomplicated satisfaction of those who know no obligation *beyond* their own satisfaction; human love yields its manifold delights, yet is always to be subordinated to the love of Him to Whom all our souls belong. The "new man" is at home in the world because it is not his Father's, and yet he has constantly to be mindful that "the fashion of this world passeth away." An

171

ambiguity affects all things earthly: they are irradiated by the light of Creation and Incarnation, yet they have to be held as always ready to be yielded up.

But these are generalities. What, in living fact, does the transmutation of self do to some of the primal realities, which are also the occasions of the most pointed questions which affect our minds and the minds of our contemporaries. And since we have talked a deal about life, let us grapple directly with the fact of *death*, in which, it is often argued, the issues of life and its meaning reach the sharpest focus.

It is not only that the New Testament documents speak of death as "the last enemy," which must be destroyed if God's will for man is finally to be done, but death is also one of the prime preoccupations of contemporary men, and of all men. Atheist existentialism, as in Jean-Paul Sartre, has rubbed it into the consciousness of modern men that it is death which finally makes nonsense of man's life: at the very moment when the whole story is ready to be told, there is no one there to hear it! But this does not mean that death should be treated frivolously, but rather that it should be taken with utmost seriousness. Life, indeed, should be lived as in the instant presence of death (at this point there is a weird convergence of Sartre and Billy Graham!). If we kid ourselves about death we kid ourselves about life, pretend a spurious meaning that in fact isn't there, and so deny ourselves the possibility of importing that precarious meaning which comes from our freedom to face and unmask the nauseating thing for what it is, and defy its power to terrorize us.

But the preoccupation with death is not an esoteric Left Bank affair. Stanford over these last two years has published an intellectual journal of high quality (the name is *Sequoia*).

I suppose that as well as anything it represents the articulate self-consciousness of the present student generation. Its first issue was constructed as follows, I was astonished to find: There was an opening article on the atomic bomb; then the life story of Thomas Heggen, author of *Mister Roberts,* who died a probable suicide; a poem called *The Death of Falstaff;* an article on the New Mexico *Penitentes* and their painful re-enactment of Calvary; and a very lovely impression of Hawaii, centered on the sea burial of a dead beach attendant. There were one or two other things in the issue, but only one or two. And I recall during this last year having a meal at one of the campus eating clubs; when it was over and I walked off across the parking lot on my way home, one of the members came hurrying after me to pluck at my sleeve in an agitated fashion: "I want to talk to you," he said, "I can't eat, I can't sleep. I've just realized that one day I have to die." Neurotic? I doubt it, for after all he *does* have to die. I think that in these days for obscure reasons latent preoccupations are coming to the surface.

Death has to be dealt with; but there is all the difference in the world between facing death in the Sartrean fashion, as a biting comment that finally shows life up for the nonsense it is, and facing death in the Christian fashion, as a real menace from which the sting has been drawn. And to understand how the sting has been drawn we have to know what put the sting there in the first place; and to understand *that* brings us very close again to the Christian understanding of the self and its overcoming. "The sting of death is sin," says St. Paul, as if death would be innocuous were it not for sin. I don't understand all that is involved here, but two things I think it does mean:

1) Death is the final irresistible attack on the citadel of

the self, which we have defended all our days. It is the self, for sinful men such as we are, in which is all our treasure; and in our anxiety to secure it we build our various defenses, our attempted securities—garrisoning it with wealth and power, burying it in sensuality, buttressing it with dogmatic certainties that brook no challenge. Anxiety is the root of sin, and this sin it is which is the sting of death; for against death there is *no* defense, and the more stake we have put in the self the more fearful we are to see its defenses finally go down.

2) Death means a finally unbalanced moral account. We make vows and break them, but always, as long as life lasts, there are new resolves to be made, only to be broken in their turn. "Hell is paved with good resolutions." But death means the end of any chance of balancing our account; it is the irrevocable debit sign on all our moral striving. As Camus puts it: "Death makes the lie definitive."

And how is the sting drawn from death? Christ heals the self's anxiety about itself by swallowing up self-love in the love of God; this alone would make death a matter of indifference, at least for ourselves. But that is not all that Christ does: he not only removes the sting from death but brings positive gifts to men, among them the gift of God which is eternal life, so that we and those we love are safely ensconced in the love of God beyond the threat of death. "Ye are dead, and your lives are hid with Christ in God." That death of the self once dead, *death shall have no dominion.* That is Dylan Thomas' great phrase, but there is a gulf fixed between his trumpet defiance of death and the Christian confidence in the face of it. Thomas' defiance is better than dumb resignation; but the Christian stance in the face of death is not that Buddhist resignation which is rooted in

174

a contempt of life, but the godly confidence which is rooted in a contempt of death.

As for the unbalanced account, Christ bears in his own body broken for us the assurance that our status in the love of God does not depend on a balance of merits over demerits. While we were yet sinners Christ died for us; and though we die as sinners, which is the only way we know how to die, there is still His overcoming both of sin and death for us, and the open gate of everlasting life.

It is when the self is emancipated from the self that it is emancipated from the fear of all its enemies, of which the last is death, and set free to serve God without fear. Something like this is what George MacLeod means by saying, "The undertaker has been and gone." Death is dead, as the self is dead, nailed on the lance of love.

THIS SIDE OF DEATH

"Blessed be the Lord God of Israel: for he hath visited, and redeemed his people . . . that we being delivered out of the hand of our enemies, might serve him without fear, in holiness and righteousness all our days." So it stands in the *Benedictus*, the Church's perennial reminder that the Christian Gospel not only takes the sting out of death but puts meaning into life this side of death. "Let me demonstrate," as the gentleman on the TV commercial is always saying.

For illustration take the vexing question of motivation for good life and for good work. A great multitude of students whom no man can number are tormented day by day by a fundamental lack of motivation. It is not long since the counseling staff at a great university called in for consultation the pious personnel. Their problem, they said, was that many

175

of the students who came to them in academic difficulty were not really short on work skills, reading skills, and the like. Their problem was one of basic motivation: "Could religion provide any resources at this point?" Now I'm not sure that even "religion" can purvey any snap solutions at this point: in the mystery of freedom there are no automatic solutions to problems that are really human. And as we saw, the profound impulse to good work and good workmanship has to be powerfully wrought into a tradition, if it is to be strongly built into the blood and bones of individual men. But short of a patient rebuilding of a Christian community and a Christian discipline of life and labor, the relevance of the Gospel both for the short and the long haul can I think be made plain.

One of the puzzling things about this question of motivation is that some of the best workers, in the academic vineyard as well as elsewere, make no profession of piety at all, while as we have seen piety is often accompanied by slovenly intellectual craftsmanship. The point to make clear here is that men *always* serve their gods (to be a self is to have a god). To put the matter too simply (for there is such a thing as disinterested scholarship, thank God, outside the Christian camp), the natural man tends to take his work seriously because he takes himself seriously, and the work is *his* work. The problem really is: how can we take our work seriously when we have ceased to take ourselves seriously? Can "pride" in work survive when the nerve of pride is cut? There is no secular answer; but in the economy of the Gospel the answer is clear, and the answer is in love. It is only love that makes us move with alacrity yet with entire disinterestedness. This is the logic of love; but since none of us is yet made perfect in love, we shall need this side of death the continu-

176

ing spurs of pride and fear and reward—until the self is perfectly subdued to the beloved Other.

We are near now to the end of our discussion of history, humanity, and the Christ. The sum of the whole matter is a curious inversion. The quest for self-understanding is self-defeating; we find ourselves only as we are sought and found by God.

> If an individual is not known to God, then he is never known as a subject, and no justice can be rendered him . . .[16]

that is, no just estimate can be made of him, either by himself or by others. And just as the quest for self-knowledge is misconceived, so the belief in the self is misplaced; self-confidence is idolatry, and the men who believe in themselves unqualifiedly are without exception in insane asylums or on the way there. Most of us are saved from that final disintegration of life because our idolatry of the self is not wholehearted.

If, then, we are not to believe in ourselves, in what or in whom *are* we to believe? In God. But who *is* God? Will any old god do, some cloudy theism, belief in "some kind of a something," a "Supreme Being"? Here again tradition comes to our aid: for it offers a frame for our thought of God, which while it is still less important than God's thought of us (we can be wrong about Him: He is never wrong about us) is still important for our thinking and our living. The doctrine of the Trinity, while it does not have the status of revelation (we say *this*, said St. Augustine, in order that we may not be silent), is yet the fruit of age-long reflection and has provided the firm bone structure on which has been built the organism of Christian truth through many centuries. C. N. Cochrane in his *Christianity and Classical Culture*[17] marks the reinvigoration which the doctrine of the Trinity brought to Hellenistic thought, as the Christian proclamation comprehended and transcended the ancient philosophic options. This is worth our attention, and provides a frame also in which we can summarize the elements of the present argument.

These Three are one God, the same in substance, equal in power and glory.[18]

I believe in one God the Father Almighty, Maker of Heaven and Earth, and of all things visible and invisible.

This is Bible talk; it is not matched anywhere, except in those traditions of faith which are rooted in the Hebrew scriptures. This creator God is not the God of the philosophers, but the God of Abraham, Isaac, and Jacob, the God of Israel. To be a Christian is to become a Jew, to "join in the tribal dance," to set oneself within an historic succession, to acquire ancestors, and to join in a common affirmation of faith and exultation, of confession and commitment. To be a self is to have a god; to be a Christian self is to take this one only living and true God for your God, or to be taken by Him to be His man, since the compulsion is the compulsion of His love.

And in one Lord Jesus Christ, the only-begotten Son of God. . . .

Here we affirm that the God who spake by the prophets, the God of the fathers, is *embodied* (Incarnate) in Christ, that history has an axis and truth a living focus, that the Divine love is not an attitude only but an Act. Here we affirm that what is wrought in Christ, the renovation of humanity, the

178

reconstitution of the human family, the taking of the sting out of death, was as an act of the living God, who here makes good on His promises and perfects His work among the children of men. And conversely: that the Christ whom historically we touch and see is not an afterthought of God, or a new God, but the same God who called Abraham and spoke by the prophets. We do not think well about God if our thought slips loose from this historic mooring, from the historic mid-point at which the Word became Flesh.

> *And I believe in the Holy Ghost,* the Lord and giver of life, who proceedeth from the Father and the Son. . . .

This affirmation is rooted in the promise of Christ, "I will send you another Comforter,"[19] and confirmed in the Church's experience of Holy Presence: the conviction born early and confirmed late in the life of the Church that Christ's living presence is independent of His presence "in the flesh" (though not independent of the fact that He was once present in the flesh) and that God does draw near to men who draw near to one another.

This triple formula has the most practical and present utility.

It delivers us from *abstractness,* from that "belief in some kind of a something" which tends to do ineffectual duty for living faith. On Trinity Sunday and every Sunday, we affirm that the God whom we worship and to whom we would have our lives subdued is not "any old god" but the God of whom it can be said that Jesus Christ is the brightness of his glory, the express image of His person.

It delivers us from *archaism,* as if the Christian faith were a mere memory of Christ, the stimulus of His example, a reverence, as a student put it to me not long ago, "for the

179

things that He stood for." For the purposes of our present argument, the doctrine of the living Spirit delivers us from a mere idolatry of tradition, as if God had nothing more and nothing new to break forth out of His word.

And it delivers us from mere *subjectivism* in religion, as if any spirit, my own unruly spirit, the spirit of piety, the spirit of the times, the spirit of the mob, were to be identified with the Holy Spirit. "You do not say 'God' by saying man in a loud voice." And here in the ageless Creed the work of the living Spirit is the extension and continuance of the work which Christ instituted in the days of His flesh, so that no man can say "Christ is Lord" save by the Holy Spirit, and conversely no man who does not say "Christ is Lord" can claim the Spirit's sanction for anything he says.

We hold to the Trinitarian formula to save us from every lesser faith than this: that when we draw together in the name of Christ the Son it is to God the Father that we draw near; and that it is the same God, the Spirit, in the heart and in the Community, who draws us together and keeps us together and leads us together into all truth.

It is *this* God with Whom we have to do: who initiates that transmutation of the self on which true selfhood depends, and Who nurtures the new self toward that true maturity, which is "the measure of the stature of the fullness of Christ."

The self is defined by its relationships, and these relationships are various. We "have to do" with things; and in that area we have dominion, we are the masters, provided we learn the technical tricks. This is the realm, if you like, of applied science, the realm in which man makes good that "dominion over the earth" which is his original endowment. But we have to do, also, with persons; and here the situation

180

is different, so different and so difficult, in fact, that we are tempted to retreat from personal encounter into a private world, or to dominate the world of persons as if persons were indeed things. For the complex and frustrating fact about persons is that, while our happiness is bound up with them infinitely more closely than it is with things, there are no technical tricks by which we can win from persons that response of love on which our very life depends. They stand equal with us, free centers of fully personal existence, not to be commanded, not to be compelled, not to be manipulated. They are open to us only as they choose to be open, they yield themselves to us only on the initiative of their free and personal will. Here, where our happiness is chiefly at stake, we have to give up all mastery of the situation and become suppliants. As persons we stand on equal terms with other persons, at their mercy as they are at ours. This is the area of contract, of covenant; we can make agreements, but we cannot make slaves without doing violence to their nature and to ours.

These two levels we know and have learned under Buber's tutelage to call the *I-It* and the *I-Thou*. We have to do with things and we have to do with persons. But the Bible speaks of Another "with whom we have to do" (Hebrews 4: 13), with Whom our relationship is of a different order entirely. He does not stand to us as one thing, among others; though superstition in religion always treats its gods as things, subject to our manipulation, subservient to our ends (and such superstition is constantly intruding itself into the Christian camp); and He does not stand to us as other persons do, on equal terms and with equal rights, with whom we can make compacts on mutually agreed terms. Jesus speaks strangely, as reported in the Fourth Gospel (John

181

15:14): He says, *Ye are my friends, if ye do whatsoever I command you.* Now this is not mutuality in any normal human sense. Friendship is normally and humanly destroyed when it is offered on terms such as that. There is implicit in Jesus' saying the claim that He is the embodiment of that Truth by which all men live, that they are their true selves only as they conform to Him and their lives are mirrored in Him. Being Who He is He can offer His friendship on no terms other than these; to do so would be to do violence not only to His claim, but to our nature.

And this, finally, is the inner meaning of the life of every man: that in point of fact man's dominion over the earth is a provisional and conditional authority; in every relationship of manipulation he is responsible to Him who made the heavens and the earth. His dominion is a responsible dominion; the sphere of man's rule is also the sphere of his obedience. He has technical mastery but no final authority, and the world will be truly and happily his only when he acknowledges that it is not his. And in our relationship with persons, while each face-to-face encounter looks like a totally free situation in which there is no curb upon those actions which may be mutually agreed, there is in each encounter a third Person present, and present with authority.

So that while the self is itself in its relationships to things and to persons, it is only truly itself in its relation of loving submission of all things and all relationships to Him. "Man's chief end is to glorify God and to enjoy Him forever."

This bondage of the self is a loving subordination which is a true emancipation, since it introduces us into that "tranquillity of order" (Augustine) which is at once the true peace and the true freedom, where our will does not beat vainly against the facts but learns that freedom which is the knowledge of necessity. The necessity in this case, however, is not simply economic or psychological necessity, but the implacable will and love of God. The condition of coming to Christian maturity, which is the likeness of Christ, requires, it would seem, the same kind of acceptance of limitations which is characteristic of any work of art. Anarchy is the enemy of art; total freedom is the enemy of life. Art is limitation: the picture has to have some relation to the frame, and to the material.

If you draw a giraffe, you must draw him with a long neck. If, in your bold creative way, you hold yourself free to draw a giraffe with a short neck, you will really find that you are not free to draw a giraffe.[20]

This is Chesterton's playful but quite serious version of our Lord's saying that "straight is the way that leadeth unto life." The end of the anarchic self is the beginning of selfhood. The English critic R. Ellis Roberts, writing somewhere of John Donne, says,

. . . always in the end his sermons come back, as a great wave covers the bare and desolate places of the shore, and he remembers his felicity as a prisoner of God, manacled by the mercies of his Saviour, saved from the dissolute liberties of eternal death.

That is the authentic accent: the false autonomy of the self which is death; the merciful bondage of Christ which is life and freedom.

The Gospel introduces us into the prison house of Christ, which strangely turns out to be the spacious world of the love and providence of God, a world so spacious and so exhilarating that we can no longer be preoccupied with the self,

183

and talk about it cannot but be boring. For here we are
known better than we can hope to know ourselves, and loved
better even than our unregenerate selves loved ourselves.
Here we need not be for ever projecting images of ourselves
for our own admiration and our peers' approval; rather we
are content to be subdued to His will and progressively con-
formed to His likeness.

> I take religion to be (said John Wesley), . . . a con-
> stant ruling habit of soul, a renewal of our minds in the
> image of God, a recovery of the divine likeness, a still-
> increasing conformity of heart and life to the pattern of
> our most holy Redeemer.[21]

The case against Christianity is immensely strong: a mixed
and muddied history, a Church which fails to live up to its
own history, far less its fundamental charter; confusion in
Christian thought and inconsistency in Christian life. But
I would almost stake the whole case on the capacity of the
Christian faith to make paradoxical sense of the problem of
our selfhood. Somewhat like this:

> If you knew that there was One greater than yourself,
> who knows you better than you can know yourself, and
> loves you better than you can love self, who can make you
> all you ought to be, steadier than your squally nature, able
> to save you from squandering your glorious life, who
> searches you beyond the standards of earth . . . if He
> were a youthful God who would understand you because
> He is ever young, yet with the wealth of the ages and eter-
> nities so that you would be always learning and never
> exhausting the store; One who gathered into Himself all
> great and good things and causes, blending in His beauty

all the enduring color of life, who could turn your dreams into visions, and make real the things you hoped were true; and if that One had ever done one unmistakable thing to prove, even at the price of blood—His own blood—that you could come to Him, and having failed come again, would you not fall at His feet with the treasure of your years, your powers, service and love? And is there not One such, and does He not call you from His cross to His cross? Is there any excuse of divided churches, inconsistent Christians or intellectual difficulty that can withstand His steady inviting gaze?[22]

"Every man has forgotten who he is. One can understand the cosmos, but never the ego: the ego is more distant than any star." I do not of myself know what I am; I do not know, as St. Paul said, what I shall be. But, said the same St. Paul, "I press on, for Jesus Christ has made me His own." That is the self identified, the self located: "Jesus Christ has made me His own."

NOTES TO CHAPTER VI

1. Calvin *Opera*. CR,V. 391–92. Beveridge translation. Quoted Harbison. *The Christian Scholar in the Age of the Reformation*. Charles Scribner's Sons, New York 1956, pp. 157–58.
2. Loew, Cornelius: *Modern Rivals to Christian Faith*. Philadelphia. The Westminster Press, Philadelphia, 1956, p. 65.
3. MacLeod, George: *Only One Way Left*. p. 41.
4. Will Herberg, in *Christianity and Society*. (reference unavailable).
5. Niebuhr, Reinhold: *The Nature and Destiny of Man*. Charles Scribner's Sons, New York, 1941, Vol. I, p. 15.

6. Niebuhr, Reinhold: *Leaves from the Notebook of a Tamed Cynic.* The Shoestring Press, Hamden, 1956, p. 83.

7. Chesterton, G. K: *Orthodoxy.* pp. 34–35.

8. *Ibid.,* p. 171.

9. Niebuhr, H. Richard: *The Meaning of Revelation.* The Macmillan Company, New York, 1946, pp. 124–25.

10. Williams, Charles: *The Descent of the Dove.* Living Age Books, New York, 1956, p. 76.

11. Ecclesiasticus 2:10.

12. *The Renewal of Man.* p. 44.

13. In *The Cardinal* (p. 363) Henry Morton Robinson has a piquant account of an Inter-faith Congress, where the delegates "were unanimous only in agreeing that bigotry and intolerance, like the grade crossing and the man-eating shark, must be eliminated." Many of us have had experiences of this kind.

14. Heim, Karl: *Christian Faith and Natural Science.* Harper & Brothers, New York, 1957, p. 211.

15. The passage is in full in Beach and Niebuhr: *Christian Ethics.* Ronald Press, New York, 1955, pp. 186–90.

16. Maritain, Jacques *Existence and the Existent.* Image Books, New York 1956, p. 84. The meaning of a longer passage is here slightly paraphrased.

17. Romans 12:3. The text is ambiguous; this reading is legitimate.

18. The Westminster Catechism.

19. The word *Comforter* refers of course to *strength (fortis)* and not first of all to *consolation.*

20. Chesterton, G. K: *Orthodoxy.* This begs some questions about the meaning of art and the varieties of painting: but the one point he makes is clear enough.

21. Quoted Beach and Niebuhr: *Christian Ethics.* Ronald Press, New York, 1955, p. 358.

22. This is a long-cherished passage from the late A. E. Whitham, one of the most attractive of English preachers. Though I cherish it I cannot locate it.

2